THE FOUR BIGGEST MISTAKES IN FUTURES TRADING

JAY KAEPPEL

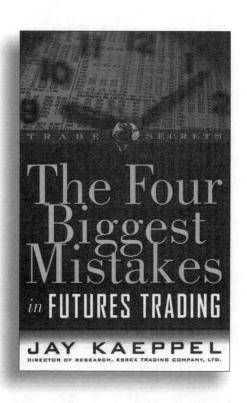

TRADE SECRETS

The Four
Biggest
Mistakes
in FUTURES TRADING

JAY KAEPPEL
DIRECTOR OF RESEARCH, ESSEX TRADING COMPANY, LTD.

This publication is designed to provide accurate and authoritative
information in regard to the subject matter covered. It is sold with
the understanding that neither the author nor the publisher is
engaged in rendering legal, accounting, or other professional service.
If legal advice or other expert assistance is required, the services of a
competent professional person should be sought.

*From a Declaration of Principles jointly adopted by a Committee of
the American Bar Association and a Committee of Publishers.*

ISBN 1-883272-08-4

Printed in the United States of America.

To Maggie, Jenny & Jimmy

Special thanks to David & Suzanne

Contents

TRADE SECRETS

INTRODUCTION

The Bad News, The Worse News, The Good News & The Better News

First the bad news: best estimates suggest that 90% of individuals who trade commodity futures lose money doing so. Now for the worse news: This estimate may be too low. The sad fact is that somewhere along the way the majority of traders make one or more critical mistakes in their trading, which cause their losses to exceed their winnings. The good news is that the mistakes that cause most losing traders to fail are quite common and readily identified. These mistakes will be detailed in this book. The better news is that by being aware of the potential for making these mistakes and by taking steps to avoid them, you can make a great leap towards becoming a more consistently profitable trader. The information contained in this book will help you to become a more successful trader – not necessarily by teaching you to be a "good" trader, but by teaching you how not to be a "bad" trader.

Why So Many Fail

To generalize using the broadest stroke possible, the high rate of failure among futures traders can be attributed primarily to three factors:

- The lure of easy money

- The lure of excitement

- An utter lack of preparedness to deal with the potential downside

Unfortunately, it seems that many individuals are lured into futures trading for a lot of the wrong reasons. To draw an appropriate analogy regarding futures markets and futures traders, consider the following scenario.

Suppose someone offered anyone who shows up the opportunity to drive an Indy race car around the track with the promise that the person with the fastest time will receive a $10,000,000 prize. Will a lot of people show up to take a shot? You bet. Will most of them be truly prepared for what they are about to do? Not likely. Will someone win the $10,000,000? Of course. Will 90% of the drivers fail to make it to the finish line?

Welcome to the exciting world of commodities speculation!

What Sets Futures Trading Apart

The staggering rate of failure among futures traders raises several extremely relevant questions:

1) What is it about futures trading that causes such a high percentage of participants to fail?

2) Is there a way to avoid the pitfalls that claim so many traders?

3) If the failure rate is so high, why does anybody bother trading futures in the first place?

What is it about futures trading that causes so many people to fail? People who have been successful in every other endeavor in life start trading futures and quickly watch the equity in their trading accounts vanish. Why is this? The answer is really very simple. It is because futures trading is unlike any other endeavor in life. If this sounds like an overstatement, rest assured it is not.

There are several factors that set futures trading apart from other forms of investment. To begin with, unlike the stock market, where rising prices can make any number of people richer, futures trading is a "zero sum" game. This means that for every dollar you make trading, somebody else is losing a dollar. If it is true that 90% of traders lose money, then we must conclude that a small minority of traders are making all the money at the expense of the vast majority. Secondly, the futures markets involve a great deal more leverage than most other types of investments. To put it into comparative terms, if the stock market were a race car, then the futures markets would be a rocket ship. While a car going 200 miles hour is certainly "fast," its speed pales in comparison to that of a rocket ship traveling 3,000 miles an hour. Finally, futures trading offers speculators the opportunity to generate spectacularly exciting rates of return, far beyond those available from other forms of investment. Maybe that is part of the problem.

Attacking From The Bottom Up Versus The Top Down

Many outstanding books have been written that focus on successful traders and how they have achieved their successes. There is much to be learned from these books. The only real problem with books that focus on successful traders is the reader can come away with a false sense of security. People may assume that by emulating the greatest traders around they can be just as successful. But is that a realistic expectation? Just because you know how someone else succeeded in a particular field of endeavor does not necessarily mean that you can duplicate his or her success. Just because you read a book about how Warren Buffet selects stocks doesn't mean that you are destined to be as good at it as he is. Yet this is how a lot of people approach investing. They read a book or look at an ad that tells them "how easy it is" to make money and later on they are that much more surprised when they find out that it is not so easy after all. There is much to be gained by learning from and attempting to emulate traders who have enjoyed a great deal of success. The danger is in assuming that you will enjoy the same type of success without paying some dues along the way.

This book takes the opposite view. Instead of focusing on the traits that allow 10% of futures traders to be successful, this book focuses on the most common and costliest pitfalls that claim the 90% of traders who lose money. Consider this the "how not to" lesson. By avoiding the mistakes detailed in this book you clear your path of the major obstacles that doom the majority of futures traders to failure.

One Word of Warning

If you are presently trading futures unsuccessfully or have done so in the past, you may be about to take a cold, hard look in the mirror and you may not like what you see. But as with anything else that might cause you to look in the mirror, the most important question to answer is not "do I like what I see?" The more important question to answer is "if I don't like what I see, am I willing to change my ways?" Generating a positive response to this question, as well as offering some guidance as to where to start, is the primary purpose of this book.

Topics To Be Covered

    I. The Four Biggest Mistakes In Futures Trading

        1. Lack of a Trading Plan

        2. Using Too Much Leverage

        3. Failure to Control Risk

        4. Lack of Discipline

    II. Why Do Traders Make This Mistake

    III. How To Avoid This Mistake

For each of the four biggest mistakes in futures trading we will first discuss what the mistake is. We will then examine and try to explain why it is so common for traders to make this mistake and why doing so causes traders to lose money. Finally, the last portion of each section will try to offer some guidance as to how an alert trader can catch himself before he makes these mistakes and how to avoid them altogether in the future.

MISTAKE #1
Lack of a Trading Plan

What is Mistake #1

Fortunately, for the purposes of illustrating Mistake #1, there is a perfect analogy. Consider the following scenario. You hear others talk of a business with low barriers to entry and in which some individuals are getting rich beyond anyone's wildest dreams. After some consideration you decide to take the plunge and engage in that business yourself. It is a fair assumption that you will begin to do some planning before engaging in that business. In fact, if you are at all prudent the chances are great that you will do a lot of planning before diving in. Furthermore, during the planning process you may learn things that you did not know at the outset that could affect your business, and you will build in contingency plans to account for these factors as well.

If you are like most people, and if you truly desire to succeed, you may find yourself becoming consumed by the depth and breadth of your planning. You may take pride in your efforts, and the extent of your preparation may help you to build confidence in yourself and your chances for success. Finally, after much soul-searching and countless hours of planning and preparation, you take the plunge and attempt to succeed in your new business. There is nothing surprising in any of this. It happens all the time and is simply the way that people go about making their fortune.

Except when it comes to futures trading.

In futures trading, a surprisingly high percentage of traders enter the markets without the slightest idea as to how they plan to succeed in the long run. Very few traders begin trading only after they have carefully thought through and planned their foray into the "exciting world of commodities speculation." Most are so anxious to get started that they just don't take the time to make the proper preparations. This phenomenon alone goes a very long way towards explaining the high rate of failure among futures traders.

Why Do Traders Make Mistake #1

The answer to the question "why do traders make this mistake" could probably apply to all of the mistakes in this book. The primary cause of Mistake #1 is simply the lure of easy money. The underlying thought seems to be "why bother wasting a lot of time planning; why not start getting rich right away?" This is understandable. There is probably not a soul on this earth who works for a living who has never once dreamed of making some huge sum of money quickly and easily and then living a life of spoiled luxury from that day forward. And the fact of the matter is that futures trading offers just that possibility (which is exactly what makes futures trading so alluring, yet so dangerous).

Consider these success stories:

- In a trading contest in 1987, Larry Williams ran $10,000 up to $1.1 million dollars in less than a year.

- Michael Marcus started with a trading account of $30,000 and over a period of years garnered over $80 million in profits.

- Richard Dennis became a legendary trader in the grain pits in Chicago in the 1970's. Starting with a reported $400, Dennis ran it up to over $200 million dollars (his father is reported to have made one of the greatest understatements of all time when he said, "Richie did a pretty good job of running up that $400 bucks").

Let's face it; these numbers are staggering. Who in their right mind wouldn't want to achieve the kind of success that these individuals have? Unfortunately, most individuals tend to focus not on the "achieving" part of the process, but rather the "post-achievement" period. In other words, if you asked the question "could you imagine having this much success trading futures," most people would not begin mentally drawing up plans as to how they would trade soybeans. Quite the opposite. Most people would start drawing up a mental laundry list of all the things they could do with the money. The "doing" part is not nearly as sexy as the "done" part.

What is missed in this kind of thinking is the reality of the situation. Like all top professionals in any business, successful traders, including the aforementioned individuals, are not lucky. They made mistakes, they paid for their mistakes, they learned from their mistakes, they learned what was required in order to succeed, and they did those things no matter how difficult they were.

- In 1973 Larry Williams published a book titled "How I Made One Million Dollars Last Year Trading Commodities" detailing his trading success that year. The next year he lost the million dollars.

- Michael Marcus started with $30,000, borrowed another $20,000 from his mother and then proceeded to lose 84% of their combined capital (imagine trying explain that to your Mom) before becoming a successful trader.

- In 1987 several commodity funds managed by Richard Dennis lost 50% of their capital and were forced to stop trading. The moral of the store is even the most successful traders suffer tremendously from time to time. You will too. The real question is "how will you react?"

One of the greatest dangers in futures trading is the danger of high expectations. By focusing optimistically on how much money he or she is going to make, a trader can easily overlook the more important task of planning out how to deal with all of the bad things that he or she will inevitably experience. If you are walking down the street and you trip and fall that is one thing. But, if you are standing on a mountaintop and you trip and fall that is something entirely different. And if you aren't even aware that you are standing on a mountaintop and you trip and fall, then the only words that apply are "look out below!" Traders who focus too much attention on how much money they might make run a very high risk of a frightening slide down a steep slope.

The Recipe For Trading Success (That Nobody Wants To Hear)

As with any other endeavor, successful futures trading requires a great deal of hard work. There is hard work involved in planning and there is hard work involved in following the plan. In the case of futures trading "hard work" more often takes the form of making and following through on difficult decisions, rather than on any type of actual physical chore. If you hope to be a successful trader you must be prepared to pay the price. The first step begins with developing a well thought out trading plan that covers all of the key elements involved.

How To Avoid Mistake #1

The only way to avoid Mistake #1 is to devote as much time, effort and energy as needed to develop a trading plan that addresses all of the key elements of trading success, all the while knowing full well that doing so does NOT guarantee your success. This daunting task moves futures trading back from the realm of fantasy squarely into the realm of reality. Your plan will serve as your road map to guide you through the twists and turns that the markets will throw at you.

There are many factors to be considered before one delves into futures trading and which need to be revisited and possibly revised as your experience and expertise grow. Yet for far too many individuals these issues are dealt with on an "as needed" basis, usually when there is money on the line, and usually when money is being lost. This is exactly the wrong time to be making critical decisions because they are more often than not based on emotion rather than on sound thinking. In developing a trading plan there are many questions to be answered and many different possible answers.

The Litmus Test

The first question to be answered is not "how should you trade futures?" The first question to be answered is "should you trade futures in the first place?" One of the keys to success in futures trading is being able to risk some amount of money which, if lost, will not adversely affect your lifestyle. In order to assess your level of readiness in this regard, you should take the following test which will tell you if you are truly prepared emotionally and financially to trade futures.

Step 1. Go to your bank on a windy day.

Step 2. Withdraw a minimum of $10,000 in cash.

Step 3. Walk outside and with both hands starting throwing your money up into the air.

Step 4. After all of the money has blown away, go home and sit down in your favorite chair and calmly say, "Gosh that was foolish. I wish I hadn't done that."

Step 5. Get on with your life.

If you actually can pass this test then you truly are prepared, both emotionally and financially, to trade futures. If you cannot pass this test then at the very least you need to go into it with your eyes wide open (you may also take some comfort in knowing that most new traders cannot pass this test at the time they start trading). Once you have decided to go ahead and trade futures there are a number of issues that need to be addressed.

How Much Capital Will You Commit To Futures Trading

If anyone asks you "what is the easiest way to make a million dollars trading futures," the answer is "start with two million." All kidding aside this is unquestionably a true statement. The more capital you can afford to lose without adversely affecting your lifestyle, the greater the likelihood that you will be successful. More initial capital affords you greater flexibility and more cushion when the inevitable bad periods occur. This is so simply because having more capital that you can afford to lose reduces your emotional attachment to the money.

Emotional attachment to money is deadly. Ask successful traders about the money in their trading account and almost always they will say "I don't think of it as money." Actually, thinking of it as money is not the worst thing. The worst situation is when a trader looks at the money in his trading account not as money, but as all of the things he could buy with that money. If you find yourself after a winning trade saying "well now I can buy this or that," or after a losing trade saying "well now I can't buy this or I can't buy that," you are in grave danger.

After you make the decision to trade futures the next step is to decide how much money you can realistically afford to risk. If you are going to open and trade your own account it is recommended that the absolute bare minimum account you should open is $10,000. A common suggestion to traders is that you should always try to limit your risk on a single trade to an absolute maximum of 5% of your trading capital (and ideally a lot less). If you open a $10,000 account this means that you can only risk $500 per trade. In most futures markets this would be considered a fairly "tight stop." So if your timing is not exactly right you will likely get stopped out on a fairly regular basis. This is another reason why "more is better" when it comes to starting capital.

Whatever amount you decide to commit, you should place the entire amount into your brokerage account. For accounts greater than $10,000 you can buy T-Bills with a portion of your capital in order to earn interest. If you decide to commit $25,000 then you should place the entire $25,000 into your brokerage account. You may also decide that if you lose say 50% of your capital, you will stop trading. This may lead some traders to say "well if I'm only going to risk $12,500 I'll just put that amount into my account." This is a mistake. In the worst case scenario it is a very different situation to be trading a $15,000 account that started out as a $25,000 account than to be trading a $2,500 account that started out as a $12,500 account. Once your account dips under a certain level your flexibility is so limited that it is essentially like piloting a plane in a death spiral. You are at the controls but you are no longer in control. One of the truest maxims in trading is "if you absolutely, positively cannot afford to lose any more money, you absolutely, positively will lose more money." Don't doubt this one for a second. Think seriously about how much you can truly afford to commit and then commit the entire amount.

What Market or Markets Will You Trade

The next decision is whether to specialize in one market or to diversify across different markets. This is a very personal choice. At first glance it would seem easier to focus all of your attention on a single market. However, there are pitfalls to such an approach. First, it is extremely difficult to always make money in any single market. So if you trade only one market and you go into a bad period of trading, you have no other avenues for offsetting your losses as you might if you were to trade a diversified portfolio of markets. Secondly, experience has shown that the majority of traders who have successfully specialized in one market are floor traders who actually "make a market" in that commodity. A little explanation is required in order to understand the benefit they enjoy.

If you want to place an order in a particular market, you can call your broker and ask for the latest "bid" and "ask" prices for that market. If you are trading September Soybeans for instance, he may tell you "the bid is 510, the ask is 510¼." This seemingly tiny spread has significant implications. What it means is that if you immediately place a market order to buy September Soybeans you will buy them at 510¼. If you immediately place a market order to sell September Soybeans you will sell them at 510. The person on the other side of this trade is the "market maker," who is the individual who sets a bid and ask level (in reality it is not just one individual). In essence, for the "privilege" of getting a fill you are giving up a $\frac{1}{4}$ point, or $12.50 on one contract in this example. In other words, if the bid and ask are 510 and $510\frac{1}{4}$ respectively, and an order to buy comes into the market, the market maker stands ready to sell at $510\frac{1}{4}$. If an order to sell comes in the market maker stands ready to buy at 510. The retail trader pays the difference between the bid and the ask and the market maker pockets the difference. In theory, the difference between the bid and ask is a risk premium intended to give market makers some inducement to assume the risk of making markets.

The purpose of this discussion regarding bid and ask prices is to illustrate why traders who successfully specialize in only one market are usually market makers and not retail traders. Simply stated, they have an "edge" by virtue of being able to buy at the bid and sell at the ask. The retail trader never buys at the bid nor sells at the ask. If you plan to be a market maker or if you truly feel you have some type of edge in a particular market, fine, just trade that market. Otherwise, it is suggested that you trade a portfolio of at least three markets.

What Type of Trading Time Frame Is Best For You

The phrase "trading time frame" refers to the length of time that you generally plan to hold trades. Will you trade short-term, long-term or somewhere in between? Also, what is your definition of short-term, long-term, etc.? This is a critical decision as each individual has a different temperament for risk. *It is essential to trade in a manner that fits your own personality.* If you have trouble holding on to a trade for more than a few days it makes little sense to use a long-term trading approach. The aforementioned market maker (buying at the bid and selling at the ask) may often hold a trade for as little as 10 seconds (buying 20 Soybean contracts at 510 and 10 seconds later selling 20 contracts at 510¼ yields a $250 profit). There are off-floor traders who trade in and out using anywhere from 1-minute to 5-minute bar charts. They are often day traders who are always flat by the end of the day. On the other end of the spectrum, there are traders who might use fundamental information or monthly bar charts to trade. These traders focus their attention entirely on long term trends. And in between there are trend-followers, counter-trend traders, traders using Gann, Elliot Wave, volatility breakouts, moving averages, etc., etc.

Day traders will tell you that day trading is the best way to trade and will give you very good reasons why they believe this is so. Trend-followers will tell you that trend-following is the only way to go, and so on and so forth. The bottom line is simply this: No matter what anyone tells you, *there is no one best way to trade.* You must identify the approach that is best suited for you personally. If you can't follow the markets all day, then it is unrealistic to expect to be a successful day trader. Let me give you a real-life example.

A pediatrician decided to day trade the S&P 500. At first, he would run back to his office between appointments and check the quote screen and perhaps make a trade, before rushing to his next appointment. As the losses began to mount he would start saying "excuse me for a minute" during appointments to go check the quotes. Eventually he started running late to appointments or would leave appointments and not come back for 5 to 10 minutes while he tried to trade his way back to profitability. Would it surprise you to learn that he lost money, stopped day trading the S&P and had to do a lot of apologizing to retain a good portion of his clientele? Probably not. In retrospect this was clearly a recipe for disaster. In this case, the lure of easy money—the idea that he would "trade in and out" a few times a day and pick up some extra cash—was so enticing to this individual that he made the mistake of not acknowledging to himself that his schedule was simply not suitable for day trading.

The purpose of this example is not to denigrate day trading (nor day-trading pediatricians). The real point is this: if you took a very successful day trader and forced him to trade only once a month using fundamental information he would no longer be a successful trader. Likewise if you took a successful long-term trend-follower and forced him to trade 15 times a day he too would be like a fish out of water and he would no longer be a successful trader. When starting out, making a well thought out decision regarding the trading time frame is critical. Also, if you have traded for awhile with little or no success it may be time to look at altering your trading approach to use a shorter or longer time frame. The bottom line is that there is no inherent advantage to trading more often or less often. *The question to be answered is simply to determine which approach works best for you.*

To get a feel for the differences in a possible trading time frame, examine Figures 1-1, 1-2 and 1-3. Each figure displays the price action of T-Bond futures over a three and a half month period. The only difference is that each depicts the trading action using a different trading system, one long-term, one intermediate-term and one short-term. On the

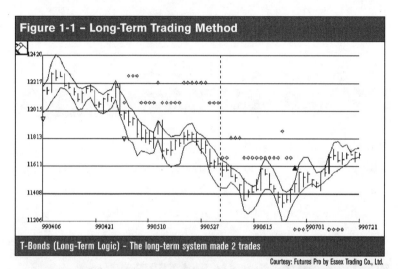

Figure 1-1 – Long-Term Trading Method

T-Bonds (Long-Term Logic) - The long-term system made 2 trades

Courtesy: Futures Pro by Essex Trading Co., Ltd.

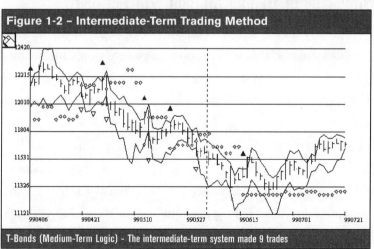

Figure 1-2 – Intermediate-Term Trading Method

T-Bonds (Medium-Term Logic) - The intermediate-term system made 9 trades

Courtesy: Futures Pro by Essex Trading Co., Ltd.

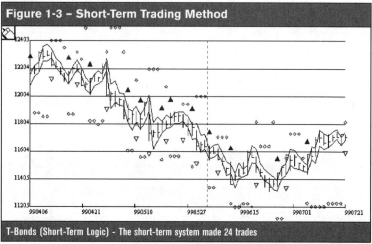

Figure 1-3 – Short-Term Trading Method

T-Bonds (Short-Term Logic) - The short-term system made 24 trades

Courtesy: Futures Pro by Essex Trading Co., Ltd.

graphs, an up arrow indicates buying, a down arrow indicates selling, and small diamonds indicate stop-loss stops. Trading the same market, the long-term system made 2 trades, the intermediate-term system made 9 trades and the short-term system made 24 trades.

What Type of Trading Method Will You Use

With the proliferation of computers, trading system development seems to have replaced stamp collecting as the hobby of choice. Trading system development is the area where a lot of traders focus the bulk of their attention. And this is not necessarily a bad thing. Using an unemotional systematic approach to trading can greatly increase your odds of success because it can remove your ego from the day-to-day decision-making process and can reduce your emotional attachment to the money in your trading account. The beauty of a trading system—which automatically generates buy and sell signals based on some preset objective criteria—is that it doesn't care what the weather is. It doesn't care if a big announcement is forthcoming, if the Fed chairman is speaking in 20 minutes nor about the price of tea in China. All it knows is that if a certain set of criteria is met it will say "buy" and if another set of criteria is met it will say "sell." In essence, it never makes a mistake. This is not to say that it won't have losing trades. It just means that it always does what it is *supposed* to do.

Compare this to the trader who flies by the seat of his pants, buying or selling short based on subjective decision making. He buys and the market goes down; he reverses to short and the market rallies. He thinks he should buy but decides to wait. The market then explodes higher and he misses the big move, the one which would have made back the losses and amassed a sizable profit. This scenario can happen to a trader using an objective trading system also. However, the difference is in the emotional aftermath.

The system trader may begin to question his system after a particularly bad period of trading, but this is a far easier position to be in than the subjective trader who just made three big mistakes back to back to back. It is hard enough to stomach losses when the markets knock you around. It is far more painful when you do it to yourself. Subjective trading involves entering into trading with the idea in the back of your head that when the time is right to enter or exit a trade "I'll just know." This approach is fraught with peril. On the other side of the coin, it should be clearly understood that utilizing a purely mechanical trading system in no way guarantees that you will be trade profitably. What it does mean is that you may be able to drag around a lot less emotional baggage than the subjective trader. A subjective trader who "makes it up as he goes along" will likely have a number of opportunities to "beat himself up" over the bad trades he has made that he shouldn't have and the great trades that he didn't take when he had the chance.

Whether you choose to trade systematically, subjectively or somewhere in between there are certain criteria that you need to address. The more clearly stated and objective your answers to these questions, the greater the likelihood of your long-term success.

What Criteria Will You Use To Enter a Trade

A systematic trader may look for some type of moving average cross-over. A subjective trader might look for a market that is starting to trend, and an astrologer may short the S&P 500 when Jupiter aligns with Mars. The possibilities are limitless. The key here is to devise some method of trade entry that has some realistic probability of generating profits. One advantage the systematic trader has is that he can formalize his trading rules, run them through the computer, and see if his method actually generated some profits in the past. This can lead to a whole other set of problems if the system developer "over optimizes" the results. With enough indicators it is possible to devise a system that fits the past almost perfectly. The bad news is that such systems almost never perform well in the future when real money is on the line. Still it is generally preferable to have some idea of what you can expect from your trading approach than to say, "well, I think my theory is really going to hold up," and to then start risking real money to prove your theory—which is essentially what a subjective trader does.

The point here is that *if you develop some set criteria for entering trades, and if you have some realistic reason to expect this criteria to generate good signals and you follow each signal as generated, you give yourself the best chance for success.*

What Criteria Will You Use To Exit A Trade With A Profit

Once you reach this stage you are starting to get into the nitty-gritty of trading. Market makers generally make only a few ticks on the majority of their profitable trades. On the other hand, long-term trend followers often need to ride major trends for a long time in order to maximize their profitability. Once again this is a personal decision but it is important to make some decisions ahead of time for several reasons. First, oddly enough, one of the most difficult things for many futures traders to do is to ride a winning trade. When you get into a trade that immediately goes in the right direction the desire to "take the money and run" can be overwhelming. It can also be a huge mistake. For example, if you are a trend following trader who generally experiences 60% losing trades, you absolutely have to have some big winners in order to offset the majority of smaller losses you incur along the way. If you take profits too soon on a regular basis you are essentially shooting yourself in the foot by doing exactly the opposite of what you need to be doing given your chosen approach to trading. (The "hard work" of trading usually involves making and sticking to difficult decisions. Fighting off the urge to cash out a winning trade when your approach tells you to hold on is a perfect example of his type of "hard work.") On the other side of the coin, if you are a counter-trend trader—selling into rallies and buying on dips—you may need to take profits more quickly before the trend turns back against you.

If you develop some objective profit-taking criteria which has a realistic probability of helping you to make money and you stick to it trade in and trade out, you are far ahead of the majority of other traders.

What Criteria Will You Use To Exit A Trade With A Loss

In the end it is not so much what you make when things go well that will decide your fate as a futures trader, but rather what you keep when things go poorly. Effectively cutting losses is generally considered to be the number one key to long-term success in futures trading. As a result, your answer to the question *"what criteria will you use to exit a trade with a loss" may have more of an impact on your ultimate success or failure as a trader than any other single factor.* If you doubt this is true then you should read (and re-read) Market Wizards by Jack Schwager. In that book Schwager interviews a number of top professional traders to get some insight into what separates them from the average trader. Several common themes are evident throughout but none more so than the need to cut losses and to keep losses small.

The truest thing that there is to know about futures trading is that there will be losing trades. There was a broker who would always discuss his "guarantee" with new clients before they made their first trade. His guarantee was this: "the only thing I can guarantee you is that there will be losing trades." Most people probably didn't care to hear this but he actually did them a favor by injecting this dose of reality into their mind-set before they got started.

Nobody likes to lose money, even on a singe trade. Yet exiting a losing trade in order to cut a loss can actually be viewed as a positive step because it serves the purpose of keeping you in the game for another round. Futures trading is not about being right. It is about being right enough at times to offset all the times you were wrong and also to never be "too" wrong. Every time a trader enters a trade he hopes to make money. When a trade starts to go the wrong way many traders take it personally and have a great deal of difficulty with acknowledging that they were "wrong." Yet one of the great ironies of futures trading is that very often the best thing that you can do is to take a loss and exit a trade before your loss becomes too big.

As with all of the other questions posed in this section there is no one right answer. You can use tight stops, you can use wide stops, you can use stops that vary depending upon volatility and so on and so forth. *The key at this stage is to select some method that you will use when you have money on the line and then stick to it once you are actually trading.*

A Word Of Advice: Adhere to the Four Cornerstones

As you develop answers to the questions that have been raised in this section, it can be helpful to have an underlying framework within which to fit the pieces. One example of such a framework can be referred to as The Four Cornerstones of Successful Trading. They are:

- Go With The Trend

- Cut Your Losses

- Let Your Profits Run

- Don't Let The Big Winners Get Away

Go With The Trend

One of the most useful skills that any trader can develop is the ability to identify a trend. If you can identify a market in an uptrend and enter a long position or identify a market in a downtrend and enter a short position, you have the potential to make a great deal of money. Too many traders spend all of their time trying to "predict" what will happen next, rather than simply focusing on answering the question "what is the trend *right now?*"

The fascination with predictions is understandable. If you could predict today where a given market will go tomorrow with any consistency you would be rich beyond your wildest dreams. Unfortunately this desire is just that, a dream. The heart of the problem seems to be that there are so many people making so many predictions that the naïve trader almost can't help but to think, "well there must be something to it. These guys on TV can't all be wrong can they?" In fact they can, just not all at once. And therein lies the fascination with predictions. If someone makes enough predictions eventually he may get one right. If a market prognosticator on TV gets a prediction right he is likely to be sought out for more predictions for a fairly long period of time, regardless of how many of his subsequent predictions actually fail to pan out.

Expecting to trade profitably in the long run by latching onto somebody's predictions or by relying on your own is simply an exercise in hope. *Successful traders learn that the ability to identify the current trend is far more useful than a thousand predictions.*

Cut Your Losses

This topic will be discussed in greater detail in Sections 2 and 3. For now simply note that the effectiveness with which you cut your losses on trades gone bad will probably have more effect on your success or failure as a trader than any other single factor.

Let Your Profits Run / Don't Let Big Winners Get Away

At first these two objectives seem to be at cross purposes. If you are holding a winning trade and you take a profit you are no longer letting your profits run. Conversely, if you are holding a big winning trade and you let it ride, then you run the risk of letting a big winner get away. So what is the right thing to do? The answer to this paradox lies in your answer to the question "what criteria will you use to exit a trade with a profit?" Whatever technique you decide upon for exiting a trade with a profit you must apply trade after trade after trade.

Constantly refer back to these four cornerstones when developing your trading plan. Doing so will help you to develop a solid approach to trading, one which has a realistic probability of making money in the long run. It will also help your confidence to know that you are building a framework which is based upon the most important concepts in successful trading.

Summary

Planning plays a key role in the success or failure of any endeavor. The more prepared an individual is when starting out the greater his likelihood of long-term success. Unforeseen problems that must be dealt with as they occur are inevitable and can cause even the best laid plans to unravel. As a result, true success in any enterprise results from laying out a well thought out plan, following the plan, adapting to unforeseen problems, and always keeping one's head above water. Futures trading is no exception.

Your trading plan will serve as your roadmap to help you through the twists and turns that the markets will throw at you. It should also serve as a constant frame of reference, particularly when things are not going well. When you encounter difficult times in trading, it is not unlike flying a plane in bad weather at night. Under such circumstances, your inner ear will lie to you and tell you that your wings are level even when they are not. In order to keep your wings level you must rely upon and trust your instruments completely. Likewise, when trading during a bad stretch your inner voice will lie to you and will tell you to do things that you normally would not, and that deep down you know you should not. But because you are losing money at the time you may be tempted to say "why not?" In order to keep your head level in such circumstances you must rely upon and trust your trading plan completely. And given that you will at times have to rely so implicitly upon your trading plan, it will hopefully be clear to you why *forming a comprehensive trading plan is your first step toward trading success.*

MISTAKE #2
Using Too Much Leverage

What is Mistake #2

Among the general public futures trading is generally considered to be a wildly speculative activity. Most people have little trepidation about moving money into stocks or bonds or mutual funds. But ask them if they have considered trading futures and they get this incredulous look on their face and say "whoa, what do you think I am, crazy?"

What is it about futures trading that has earned it such a disreputable reputation? The common perception among the general public seems to be that the individual markets themselves—whether it be Silver, Soybeans or Natural Gas—are wildly volatile and that volatility is what causes most traders to lose money. While there is no question that futures markets can be volatile at times, the markets themselves are not nearly as volatile as many people think, and it is not the volatility of the markets that causes the majority of problems. *What causes most of the problems is the amount of leverage used when trading futures.* This fact is not widely recognized, however. Before illustrating this let's consider what causes futures prices to rise or fall.

The price of a stock tends to rise or fall based upon the company's earnings per share, or more accurately, on the public perception of that company's earnings outlook. Conversely, the price of a physical commodity moves based upon supply and demand for that product, or more accurately, the perceived supply and demand for that product. For example, if there were a terrible drought in the Midwest the general perception would likely be that growing conditions are bad and that farmers will not be able to grow as many Soybeans as usual. Thus, based on perceptions of lower supply, the price of Soybean futures could be expected to rise. Likewise if growing conditions were perfect and supply was expected to be great, Soybean prices would likely fall. Now let's consider the volatility of the markets themselves.

The first thing to understand is that there is nothing about a bushel of Soybeans or an ounce of Gold that make them inherently more volatile or more risky than a share of stock in IBM or any other tradeable security. In fact, in terms of raw volatility (i.e., the average annual price movement as a percentage of current price), commodity prices tend to fluctuate less than stock prices. Figure 2-1 shows the historical volatility of a group of stocks and futures markets. While this is admittedly a very small sample, note that the average volatility for the stocks in this list is greater than the average volatility for the futures markets in the list. So what's going on here? Does the investing public have it backwards? Are futures really less volatile, and by extension less risky than stocks? Well, not exactly.

Figure 2-1 – Stock Volatility versus Futures Market Volatility			
STOCK	VOLATILITY %	FUTURES	VOLATILITY %
ABBOTT LABS	36.7	CATTLE FEEDER	8.7
AMER EXPR	41.1	CATTLE LIVE	14.6
AMGEN	45.3	COCOA	40.3
ANALOG-DEVICES	59.3	COFFEE	65.1
APPLIED-MATERIA	58.5	COPPER	28.2
ASA	41.5	CORN	24.5
ATMEL	68.9	COTTON	23.8
BANC ONE CORPOR	37.8	CRUDE OIL	35.4
BANKAMERICA	39.2	DJ FUTURES	13.3
BARRICK-GOLD	50.1	DOW FUTURES	23.9
BIOGEN	45.8	GOLD	34.1
BOEING	34.9	HEATING OIL	37.2
CABLETRON SYSTE	76.6	HOGS LIVE	36.0
CCUBE	57.6	LUMBER	35.2
CHASE MANHATTAN	38.0	NYFE	13.3
CIRRUS LOGIC	78.7	S&P FUTURES	17.5
CISCO SYSTEMS	44.4	S&P MINI	19.8
CMG-INFO-SERVIC	68.7	SILVER	30.0
COMPAQ	52.1	SOY MEAL	29.6
COMPUWARE	67.5	SOY OIL	25.8
CONSECO	55.4	T-BONDS	8.9
CREE RESEARCH	67.7	TNOTE5	4.4
CYPRESS-SEMI	78.0	UNLEADED GAS	33.0
DELL COMP	53.0	WHEAT	26.4
AVERAGE STOCK	54.0	AVERAGE FUTURES	26.2

Understanding Leverage

The purpose of the previous example is to illustrate that the key difference between stock trading and futures trading is not the volatility of the underlying tradeables. The key difference between trading stocks and trading futures is the amount of capital required to enter a trade and the resultant percentage return on investment. This can best be illustrated with an example. First let's consider stock trading. In order to buy $100,000 worth of IBM stock Investor A must put up $100,000 in cash (you can buy IBM stock on margin. To do so you would put up $50,000 in cash giving you 2-for-1 leverage. However, for the purposes of our example, we will forego margin buying). If Investor A puts up $100,000 cash to buy $100,000 of IBM stock and IBM stock rises 3%, Investor A will make 3% on his investment. If IBM stock declines 3% he will lose 3% on his investment. Pretty straightforward. Now let's consider a futures trade.

Each futures contract has a standardized contract size. When you buy a Soybean contract you are buying the right to purchase 5,000 bushels of Soybeans. For Soybeans a one cent move ($0.01) is worth $50. Now let's do some math. Let's say Soybeans are presently trading at a price of $5.00 a bushel. With a current price of $5.00 a bushel, the contract is currently trading for the equivalent of 500 cents. 500 cents times $50 a cent means that you would be purchasing $25,000 worth of Soybeans. Thus, if Investor B buys four Soybean contracts at $5.00 a bushel he is buying $100,000 worth of Soybeans. Now here comes the key difference between trading stocks and trading futures: to purchase (or to sell short) a futures contract a trader does not need to put up cash equal to the full value of the contract. Instead, he need only put up an amount of money which is referred to as a "margin."

Minimum margins are set by the futures exchanges and may be raised or lowered based on the current volatility of a given market. In other words, if a particular market becomes extremely volatile, the exchange on which it is traded may raise the minimum margin. As this is written, the amount of margin required to trade one Soybean contract is $750. So in order to buy $100,000 worth of Soybeans, Investor B in our example must buy four contracts at $5.00 a bushel (500 cents x $50/cent x four contracts). However, unlike Investor A who had to pony up $100,000 cash in order to buy his IBM stock, Investor B need only put up $3,000 of margin ($750 per contract x four contracts) in order to make his trade. *And therein lies the quality that makes futures trading a highly speculative endeavor—leverage.*

If IBM stock rises 3%, Investor A will make 3% on his investment. If Soybeans rise 3%, from $5.00 to $5.15, Investor B will make a 100% return on his investment (15 cents x $50 per cent x four contracts = $3,000). So what we are talking about in this example is the difference between 1-to-1 leverage versus 33-to-1 leverage. When you boil it all down, it is this leverage which gives futures trading its great upside potential as well as its frightening downside risk. If IBM declines 3%, Investor A will lose 3% on his investment. If Soybeans fall 3% from $5.00 to $4.85, Investor B will lose 100% of his investment (-15 cents x $50 per cent x four contracts = -$3,000).

Leverage is the double-edged sword that makes a few people very rich and upon which the majority of futures traders fall.

Very few individuals have the stomach to trade with leverage of 33-to-1. More unfortunately many traders do not clearly understand that they are using this kind of leverage when they trade futures. Those in the greatest danger are the ones who read about "how to make a fortune in Soybeans for just $750!," or "how you can control $25,000 worth of Soybeans for just $750." Also, *some traders are unaware that futures trading involves unlimited risk*. If you enter the aforementioned Soybean trade, buying four contracts at $5.00/bushel, your initial margin requirement is $750 a contract, or $3,000. Based on their prior experience in stocks or mutual funds or even options, some traders mistakenly assume that this is all they can lose. Not so. If Soybeans happened to trade down lock limit ($0.30/day) just two days in a row, this trader would be sitting with a loss of $12,000 ($0.60 x $50/cent x four contracts) and counting. This illustrates the importance of having a "cushion" and not "trading too big" for your account. The phrase "trading too big" can be defined as the act of trading with more leverage than is prudent given the size of your trading account and your own tolerance for risk.

Why Do Traders Make Mistake #2

Unfortunately, the blunt answer to the question "why do traders use too much leverage" is "ignorance." This is not to imply that everyone who trades futures is ignorant (although there are those who might debate this). What it means is that many traders are unaware of the amount of leverage involved. Too many traders get into futures trading without realizing or understanding the amount of leverage involved. People who trade stocks for years (putting up $1 of cash to buy $1 of stock) often mistakenly assume that they are doing the same thing with futures. They simply don't realize that when they put up $1 they may actually be buying or selling $33 worth of the underlying commodity. Few people are prepared to deal with 33-to-1 leverage. To make matters worse, those who don't even realize they are using 33-to-1 leverage have almost no hope of surviving. It is sort of like taking a test drive in an Indy race car. You know it can go fast so you prepare yourself a little, but you are used to driving the family sedan whose top speed might be 80 miles an hour. So you strap yourself in, put your foot on the gas and suddenly find yourself hurtling down the track at 220 miles per hour. The odds of your avoiding a serious accident are slim. And so it is, too, for the unenlightened futures trader.

Another problem is that there are few warnings given regarding how much leverage is too much. Brokerage houses make money based upon the number of trades made so they don't have a great incentive to tell somebody "you're using too much leverage; you should trade less." Another problem is that although there have been many good books written regarding money management, there remains no standard method for determining the proper amount of leverage to use when trading futures.

How To Avoid Mistake #2

The antidote for using too much leverage is referred to as proper "account sizing." Account sizing simply refers to a process whereby a trader attempts to arrive at the "right" amount of leverage for him. The goal is to strike a balance. You want to use enough leverage to be able to generate above average returns without using so much leverage that you expose yourself to too much risk. *The ultimate goal of sizing an account is to limit any drawdowns in equity to a percentage amount which will not be so large that it causes you to stop trading.* In order to do so you must prepare yourself as much as possible both financially and emotionally for the magnitude of drawdown you are likely to experience using your chosen approach to trading.

There is no one best way to arrive at the "perfect" amount of capital to use to trade a given portfolio. There are, however, several key factors to take into account. The ideal method is to develop a portfolio of markets and trading methods, figure out the proper amount of capital needed to trade each market, and then allocate that much capital into your trading account. From a practical point of view most traders do not have this luxury and must approach the problem from the other end. In other words, most traders don't say "here is the optimum portfolio and the required amount of capital to trade it so let me just write a check to my broker for this amount." Most traders say "I have x-number of dollars to commit to futures trading. What can I do with it?" If your optimum portfolio requires $50,000 to trade (according to the methods we will discuss in a moment) but you only have $25,000 with which to trade, you must either alter your optimum portfolio or save up another $25,000.

Assuming you are going to trade a diversified portfolio of markets, the first step is to build a test portfolio and look at the historical trading results for each individual market using the trading approach you have selected. What you want to accomplish is to arrive at a reasonable amount of capital to have in your account in order to trade one contract of each market. If possible, you will also want to consider the performance of the portfolio as a whole, to determine if more or less capital is required. In order to obtain the most useful results it is best if you have some method available to generate a trade listing for each market that you intend to trade using the approach you have chosen. It is also helpful to be able to analyze monthly profit and loss data for the portfolio as a whole. If you have actually been trading for a while you may be able to use your past monthly statements to obtain the necessary data.

The Role of Mechanical Trading Systems

There are several benefits to be gained by using a mechanical approach to trading. First, doing so can eliminate a vast array of emotional and psychological issues by virtue of the fact that you are relieved of the burden of having to subjectively make trading decisions on a day-to- day basis. The other key benefit is that by formalizing rules and testing them over past data you can arrive at an objective estimate of the expected risks and rewards. This information can be used to estimate your trading capital requirements. In order to get the most out of the approach to be described you should be using some type of mechanical system for which you can generate either hypothetical or actual trading results, or some combination of the two.

Determining The Amount of Capital Required to Trade One Market

The following discussion is not intended to offer the definitive method for arriving at a proper capital requirement for trading a given portfolio of futures markets. It does, however, address several key factors that should be considered when determining your capital requirements.

Single Market Factor #1: Optimal *f*

In his 1990 book titled *Portfolio Management Formulas*, Ralph Vince popularized a formula known as optimal f. The theory behind this method is that:

- There is a "correct" amount of capital to apply to any contract using a particular trading approach.

- Trading using the "correct" amount of capital will maximize the profitability experienced without sustaining a total loss of capital.

- Trading with less than the suggested amount of capital will likely result in a total loss of capital.

- Trading with more than the suggested amount of capital will result in an exponential decrease in the percentage return compared to using the "correct" amount.

In brief, using a listing of actual and/or hypothetical trades generated by trading one market using a given approach, a calculation is performed and a value is arrived at between .01 and 1.00. The largest losing trade within the listing of trades is then divided by this value to arrive at the suggested amount of capital with which to trade one contract.

As an example, if the largest losing trade within a particular trade listing was $2,000 and the optimal *f* value turns out to be 0.40, then the suggested capital amount would be $5,000 ($2,000 / 0.4). According to this theory, if you were only going to trade one contract of this one market using this one trading approach, then you should place $5,000 into your trading account. If future results mirror past results your percentage rate of return will be maximized by trading with $5,000. Also, according to the theory, if you trade with less than $5,000 you will likely "tap out" and if you trade with more than $5,000 you may trade profitably. However, your rate of return will be far inferior than if you had traded with $5,000. Needless to say this is a bold theory.

This approach makes the assumption that future trading results will be similar to past results. If future results are far inferior to past results then the end result using optimal f can be disastrous. However, in testing using trading systems that have a positive expectation, and for which future results were similar to past results, optimal f has definitely shown the ability to increase profits exponentially compared to simply trading a preset number of contracts. Unfortunately, the reality of the situation is that using optimal f to trade one market is generally not practical. The big problem with a strict usage of optimal f is that it does not consider drawdowns in its analysis. The only measure of risk that is used is the single largest losing trade. While the case can be made that this is statistically correct, the fact of the matter is that using this method alone will invariably result in large percentage drawdowns at some point in time. Because the drawdowns that can result on a single market basis can be huge in percentage terms, most traders will not adhere to this approach long enough to enjoy the expected benefits. However, the good news is that this method can be very useful when applied across a portfolio of markets.

Calculating Optimal *f*

The method for calculating optimal *f* is fairly complex; however, the following example should give you enough information to utilize this method if you so desire. In order to calculate optimal *f* you need a trade listing for a given market containing at least 30 trades. This approach uses an iterative process to arrive at a value of *f* between .01 and 1 that maximizes a variable known as the Terminal Wealth Relative (TWR) for a given set of trades. The profit or loss for each individual trade is divided by the largest losing trade. Then the negative of this ratio is multiplied by a factor, known as *f*, and added to 1 to arrive at a return value, referred to as holding-period return (HPR). The formula for one trade is:

PR = (-(profit or loss on trade x) / largest losing trade)
HPR on trade x = 1 + [*f* times (PR)]

This process is repeated for all trades in the trade listing. The HPR values for all trades are then added together to arrive at another value known as the TRW. The value for *f* between .01 and 1.00 that results in the largest TWR is the *f* value to be used in the final calculation. In the final calculation the largest losing trade is divided by *f* to arrive at the suggested amount of trading capital. This process is then repeated for each market in your portfolio to arrive at suggested trading capital amounts for each based on optimal *f*.

Single Market Factor #2: Largest Overnight Gap

When a futures market starts trading on a given day it is very rare that trading opens exactly at the price at which it closed the day before. Usually the opening range of prices is above or below the prior day's close. This is commonly referred to as the "opening gap." Generally opening gaps are not large. However, every once in a while something happens between the time the market closes one day and opens the next which causes prices to gap sharply higher or lower on the opening. It is extremely important to understand the implications of such events. If a market gaps sharply lower one day it means that every trader who was long as of the close the prior day suffers a big hit immediately upon the start of trading. It is important to be aware that these gaps can occur and of the potential magnitude of these moves. Unfortunately, the common response to such a possibility is "that probably won't happen to me." This is not the proper response. The proper response that the winning trader will consider is "what if this *does* happen to me?" Asking and answering this question allows you to be prepared for just such an event.

Immediately prior to the outset of the Gulf War, the common thinking was that if a messy war in the Middle East were to unfold, the price of Crude Oil would skyrocket based on great uncertainties regarding the supply of oil. On January 16, 1991, Crude Oil, traded on the New York Mercantile Exchange (NYMEX), closed at $30.29 a barrel. That night the U.S. and its allied forces unleashed a furious and highly successful air raid on Iraq which immediately raised the potential for a quick victory. The next morning the first trade for Crude Oil took place at $22.79 a barrel. This equates to a gap opening of $7.50 a barrel, or $7,500 a contract. Consider what happened in an instant when Crude Oil opened for trading that day.

Everyone who was short Crude Oil at the previous close was instantly $7,500 per contract richer. Everyone who was long Crude Oil at the previous close was instantly $7,500 per contract poorer.

Will Crude Oil ever experience another gap that big? There is no way to predict the answer to this question. It may or may not some day experience an even bigger gap. What is important is to realize that if such a move happened once it can certainly happen again. So you must prepare yourself for this possibility. If you are long a Crude Oil contract at today's close and it opens $7.50 a barrel lower tomorrow, how will you react? And more importantly, will you survive?

Table 2-1 displays the largest overnight gap in dollars for a number of futures markets. Some markets such as grains and interest rates have daily limits. For instance, a limit move for T-Bonds is 3 full points, or $3,000 per contract. So if T-bonds closed one day at 100, on the next trading day they could trade as low as 97 and/or as high as 103, but not beyond these two prices. A daily limit move for Soybeans is $0.30 or $1,500. However, if Soybeans have three limit moves in a row in the same direction then the limit for the next day expands to $0.45 or $2,250 per contract. The good news regarding markets with daily price limits is that you can only lose so much money in a single day. The bad news is that you may be "locked in" to position with no way to exit if that market moves lock limit against you. Also, in the worst case scenario a limit move one day can beget another limit move the next day. This can cause losses far in excess of what you might have expected.

Table 2-1	
MARKET	**LARGEST GAP IN $**
British Pound	$3,988
Canadian Dollar	$1,550
Cattle (Feeder)	$878
Cattle (Live)	$712
Cocoa	$1,510
Coffee	$13,838
Copper	$2,642
Corn	$1,475
Cotton	$1,940
Crude Oil	$7,500
Eurodollar	$5,525
Gold	$5,040
Heating Oil	$8,450
Hogs (Live)	$864
Japanese Yen	$5,938
Lumber	$1,776
Municipal Bonds	$2,969
NYSE Index	$11,685
Orange Juice	$3,088
Platinum	$2,025
Pork Bellies	$2,812
S+P 500 Index	$14,928
Silver	$5,105
Soybean Meal	$1,520
Soybean Oil	$906
Soybeans	$2,412
Sugar #11	$3,898
Swiss Franc	$3,062
T-Bonds	$3,000
T-Notes 10 Yr	$3,000
T-Notes 5 Yr	$1,062
U.S. Dollar	$2,330
Unleaded Gas	$7,694
Wheat	$2,412
Natural Gas	$3,870

Other markets have no daily limits. The bad news regarding trading markets with no limits is that there is no way to know if and when the previous records shown in Table 2-1 might be exceeded. Nor is there any way to predict if you will be on the right or wrong side of such a move. This is why it is important to acknowledge that such a move is possible, that you could be on the wrong side of that move and to appreciate the negative effect it could have on your trading account.

The purpose of carefully examining the largest overnight gaps shown in Table 2-1 is twofold. The first is to inject a sobering dose of reality into anyone who thinks that trading futures is going to generate easy profits. The second is to get a handle on just how much capital you realistically need in order to trade a given market.

Single Market Factor #3: Maximum Drawdown

One of the key variables that most traders focus on when considering a system to trade a particular market is referred to as the "maximum draw-down." This value represents the biggest decline in equity from any peak to the subsequent trough. It basically tells you how bad things would have gotten had you started trading at exactly the worst possible time. For example, consider the following scenario: A system trading the Japanese Yen accumulates $15,000 in profits. It then loses $10,000 before gaining another $15,000 in trading profits. In analyzing these results, we would say that the net profit was $20,000 and that the maximum drawdown was $10,000. In other words, if you had started trading at the worst possible moment (just after the first $15,000 in profits had been made), you would have had to sit through—and continue to trade through—a loss of $10,000 before getting back into the black. This is a critical piece of information. If you know there is no way you would continue to keep trading in the face of a $10,000 drawdown, then you should not trade this particular market using this particular approach.

One important attribute of the maximum drawdown value is that it is specific to the trading method that you are using. As a result it provides another useful piece of information in determining how much capital you realistically need in order to trade a given market using the method you have chosen.

One word of warning regarding maximum drawdown analysis: Previous records are made to be broken. Just because the trading method above has so far experienced a maximum drawdown of $10,000, this in no way implies that it will not experience an even larger drawdown in the future. This is especially true if you are analyzing highly optimistic hypothetical results. However, because the future is unknowable we have little choice but to use past results as a proxy for the future. In this case we are at least making some attempt to acknowledge the worst case scenario experienced to date and to factor that into our trading capital requirements.

One Caveat to Analyzing Trading System Results

In Section 1 we touched upon the dangers of "over-optimizing" a trading system. If you use enough indicators and filters and data and crunch enough parameter values you can arrive at a system that shows phenomenal results when back-tested over historical data, and that has almost no chance of working in the real world. Just because a given set of indicators and values fit past data well, it does not mean that it will fit future data well. Likewise if you are using the results of a highly curve fit, over-optimized system to determine capital requirements the results are easy to predict—low recommended capital requirements and huge real-time drawdowns far in excess of what was expected.

When developing a trading system it is recommended that you use part of your database to develop the system and then test the system over different data that was not included in the original development process. This is referred to as "out-of-sample" testing. While still not the same as real live trading, testing using out-of-sample data is one way to estimate how your system might perform when you start to trade it with real money. Also, because the trading results are almost always less using out-of-sample data than when using data included in the optimization process, out-of-sample data is much more useful for determining realistic trading capital requirements.

Arriving at a Suggested Dollar Value Per Contract

One simple approach to arriving at a suggested amount of capital to have in your trading account in order to trade one contract of a given market using a particular systematic approach is to add up the three values just discussed and divide the sum by 3. The formula is as follows:

(Optimal f in \$ + Largest Overnight Gap in \$ +
(Maximum Drawdown in \$ + Margin Requirement)) / 3

For example, let's say that you are looking to trade the Japanese Yen with a system you have developed. The optimal f value is \$3,457, the largest overnight gap for the Yen to date has been \$5,938, the maximum drawdown in testing using your system was \$4,124 and the margin requirement for one Japanese Yen contract is \$3,000. You can then plug these values into the formula to arrive at a suggested amount of capital:

(\$3,457 + \$5,938 + (\$4,124+\$3,000)) / 3 = \$5,506

For this example, it is suggested that you have at least \$5,506 in your trading account in order to trade one Japanese Yen contract using this system.

This method takes into consideration three valuable pieces of information regarding your specific trading method in trading a particular market. Optimal f uses a scientific math-emat-ical process to arrive at the amount of trading capital that should theoretically maximize your profitability if future results are similar to past results. Including the largest over-night gap for the market in question and the maximum draw-down using your approach to trade this market forces you to take into account previous worst-case scenarios.

If you cannot calculate an optimal f value you may wish to substitute an old standby rule of thumb value which is arrived at by multiplying the initial margin requirement for that contract times three. One reason for using optimal f is because the value it arrives at takes into account the actual performance of the system you are using. If your system is very good, optimal f will indicate that you can trade it with less capital than if your system is not as good. Using margin times three results in the same suggested amount of capital regardless of the performance of the system used.

Using margin requirement times three is an acceptable rule of thumb. However, in order to appreciate its limitation consid-er two traders who are both presently long T-Bond futures traders. Trader A uses an excellent systematic approach that consistently generates profitable annual returns while Trader B pretty much makes it up as he goes along. Is the risk the same for both traders? Herein lies something of a paradox. For any given trade the answer is "yes." However, in the long run the answer is almost certainly "no." By virtue of using a superior approach to trading, Trader A has a greater likeli-hood of success and should be able to commit less capital than Trader B.

If you do not have any way to back test your system then the suggested formula for calculating a reasonable amount of capital to trade one contract of a given market is:

((Initial margin * 3) + Largest Overnight Gap in $) / 2

For the Japanese Yen the initial margin requirement (at the time this is written) is $3,000 and the largest overnight gap has been $5,938. According to this formula the suggested capital requirement would be:

(($3,000 * 3) + $5,938) / 2 or $7,469

These formulas are intended to help you determine the absolute minimum amount of capital you should have in your trading account in order to trade your desired portfolio.

Arriving at an "Aggressive" Suggested Account Size

Once you have constructed a portfolio of markets and have calculated the suggested amounts to trade one contract of each on a market-by-market basis, it is a simple step to arrive at a suggested amount for the entire portfolio. Simply add up the individual amounts calculated in the previous step for each contract. Say you plan to trade the Japanese Yen, T-Bonds, Soybeans and Natural Gas and the suggested capital requirement for each using the formulas just discussed are $5,506 for the Yen, $5,982 for T-Bonds, $5,076 for Soybeans and $4,241 for Natural Gas. By adding these values together we find that in order to trade one contract of each market you should have at least $20,805 in your trading account. This should be a considered a minimum account size for trading this portfolio. Adding more money to the account beyond this amount will reduce your percentage rate of return. However, it will also reduce your drawdowns as a percentage of trading capital and will give you more staying power when the inevitable drawdowns occur.

Arriving at a "Conservative" Suggested Account Size

If you are able to calculate or at least estimate monthly returns from your portfolio it is possible to arrive at what can be referred to as a "conservative" account size. In calculating a "conservative" account size for the portfolio in the previous example, please note that neither the portfolio nor the dollar amount of profit or loss changes. What changes is the amount of capital committed to trading that portfolio, the percentage rate of return and the drawdown as a percentage of account equity. By using more capital we can effectively reduce the magnitude of any drawdowns on a percentage basis to a tolerable level.

To use this method it is advisable to have at least 30 months of data. When performing mathematical analysis at least 30 elements are required in order to generate statistically meaningful results. To use this method:

- First add up all of the monthly profit/loss figures and divide by the number of months considered in order to calculate the average monthly dollar profit for the portfolio as a whole.

- Calculate the standard deviation of monthly returns (See Appendix A for the mathematical formula for calculating standard deviation).

- Multiply the standard deviation of monthly returns by 3 and then divide the result by 0.1.

For a given set of data, a one standard deviation move above and below the average encompasses ⅔rds of the data under consideration. A two standard deviation move above and below the average includes 96% of the data and a three standard deviation move above and below the average includes 99% of the data. By multiplying the standard deviation of monthly returns by three we arrive at a dollar figure that encompasses 99% of all previous monthly gains or losses. By dividing this value by .1, we are attempting to insure that there is a 99% chance that you will not experience a monthly loss in excess of 10%. This assumes of course that future results will be similar to past results.

Let's say that the standard deviation of monthly returns for our earlier example portfolio is $1,500. We multiply this value by three to arrive at $4,500 and then divide this value by 0.1 to arrive at a suggested "conservative" account size of $45,000. If future results are similar to past results, then by trading this account with $45,000 there is a 99% probability that we will not experience a monthly drawdown in excess of 10% (or $4,500 in this case).

Arriving at an "Optimum" Suggested Account Size for Your Portfolio

To arrive at what we will refer to as the "optimum" account size for a given portfolio, simply add together the "conservative" account size and the "aggressive" account size and divide by two. This is the amount of capital you should ideally consider having in your account before trading that particular portfolio. For the example that we have been using, the aggressive account size is $20,805 and the conservative account size is $45,000. To arrive at the "optimum" account size for this portfolio we simply add these two values together and divide by two. By adding $20,805 to $45,000 and dividing by two we arrive at an "optimum" account size of $32,903.

Digging a Little Deeper

Assuming you have all the required data there is some useful information you can glean by analyzing monthly returns. Ideally you will have at least 30 months of real-time and/or hypothetical monthly data to examine. Using the formulas below can help you to estimate what you can realistically expect from your portfolio in terms of risk and reward.

A) **Expected Annual % Return** = Average monthly % return compounded over 12 months. For our example portfolio, the average monthly return is $729 or 2.2% of $32,903. By compounding this monthly return over 12 months we can estimate an average annual return of 30.8%.

B) **Expected maximum drawdown in $** = Standard Deviation of monthly returns x 4. The standard deviation in monthly return for our example port folio is $1,500, so we should be prepared to sit through a maximum drawdown of $6,000. In other words, any drawdown we experience which is less than $6,000 must be considered "normal" for our account using our chosen approach.

C) **Expected maximum drawdown in %** (Expected maximum drawdown in $ / Account Equity) - $6,000 / $32,903 = 18.2%.

D) **P/L / Standard Deviation Ratio** = Average monthly % return / standard deviation of monthly returns. For our example portfolio P/L = $729 and Standard Deviation = $1,500, so this ratio is 0.49. Anything above 0.5 is outstanding.

E) **Expected Profit / Drawdown Ratio** = (A / C) – What you are looking for is enough upside to justify the expected volatility. The minimum ratio to consider would be 1-to-1. For our example port folio A= 30.8 and C = 18.2, so E = (30.8/18.2) or 1.69. Anything above 1.5 is outstanding.

F) **% of Profitable 3-Month Periods** – For our example portfolio, 79.8% of all 3-month periods have been profitable.

G) **% of Profitable 12-Month Periods** – For our example portfolio, 98.3% of all 3-month periods have been profitable.

A high percentage of profitable 3-month and 12-month periods is a major plus from a psychological standpoint. A trader is far more likely to continue trading using a given approach if he experiences a high percentage of profitable 3- and 12-month periods.

Summary

When an account goes into a drawdown, the longer it takes before a new equity high is achieved, the greater the likelihood of a trader "pulling the plug" prematurely. The most important consideration is to make a realistic assessment of whether or not you will be able to continue trading in the face of a drawdown, which this analysis suggests, is "normal" for this portfolio. If you are prepared to keep trading through a 20% drawdown, but this analysis suggests that the expected maximum drawdown is 30%, you have a critical piece of information. You need to either allocate more capital to your trading or make some changes to your portfolio. The implication here is that you will probably not enjoy the Expected Annual % Return because it is likely that at some point your maximum drawdown "pain threshold" will be exceeded and you will stop trading.

Determining the proper capital requirements for trading a given portfolio is a difficult and often overlooked task. Many traders put what they think they can afford to lose into a trading account, pick a few markets that they like and start trading, with little or no analysis regarding the kind of volatility and drawdowns they might expect to encounter along the way. Unfortunately, *the impact of failing to carefully consider capital requirements for trading a given portfolio can be disastrous.* Applying the steps in this chapter can help you to avoid the mistake of using too much leverage.

MISTAKE #3
Failure to Control Risk

What is Mistake #3

If you were going to engage in some highly risky activity other than futures trading you would likely spend a fair amount of time planning out how to avoid the associated pitfalls. For instance, if you were going to go sky diving it is probably a safe bet that prior to the jump you would check and recheck your parachute almost to the point of obsession. However, as I said earlier, futures trading is unlike any other endeavor. In futures trading it is not uncommon to see people run out the airplane door without even looking to see if they *have* a parachute. These traders usually fall into the category of new traders who are hoping to make "easy money." However, even veteran traders who should know better occasionally fail to keep their guard up. And when they do they pay dearly. Make no mistake about the vicious nature of futures markets. If you make a mistake, and leave yourself exposed for one moment, the markets can reach out and knock you flat. If you don't believe me, ask Victor Neiderhoffer.

Victor Neiderhoffer was a highly successful futures trader for years (his managed accounts averaged a 31% annual return over a 13-year period) and the author of the best-selling book "The Education of A Speculator." In October 1997, the fund run by Mr. Neiderhoffer was short a large quantity of S&P 500 put options (which means he would lose money if the market fell). The market had been declining and Mr. Neiderhoffer believed the market was due to bounce back quickly. On October 27, the Dow Jones Industrial Average fell over 500 points in a single day. Because he still felt he was correct that the market would bounce back soon Mr. Neiderhoffer did not cover his naked put positions. In one of the greatest ironies in futures trading history, he was in fact correct and the market started to bounce back the very next day. That was the good news. The bad news was that by the time that happened his fund was out of business. When the positions were marked-to-market at the close of trading on October 27, 1997, the fund was allegedly some $20 million dollars in the hole. The fund's clearing firm closed out all the positions (just before the market turned around) and their people contacted Mr. Neiderhoffer's people to discuss how to make good on the slight $20 million deficit.

The moral of the story:
risk control in futures trading is NEVER optional.

Why Do Traders Make Mistake #3

The sad fact of the matter is that the majority of traders don't get around to addressing money management issues until after they have suffered an unexpectedly large decline in equity.

Part of the reason for this is that when a trader starts a new trading program his primary focus is the upside potential and not the downside risk. Very few people get into futures trading simply to diversify their investments. And almost no one gets into futures trading hoping to generate an 8% average annual return. The only reason to venture into something as risky as futures trading is to earn above average rates of return (You don't see people getting into Indy race cars to drive to the corner market. The only reason to drive one is to go fast). Unfortunately, because so many traders are focused on the "upside potential" there is a dangerous tendency to either ignore or at least downplay the downside risk. In essence, too many traders "want to believe" that they will be successful or they buy into the idea that futures trading can generate "easy money." These are extremely dangerous notions.

In reality, most traders would benefit from "fearing" the markets more than they presently do. A fear of losing a large chunk of money quickly is what causes traders to keep their guard up. A lack of fear is what gets them into trouble. In almost every other endeavor we are taught to "fight, fight, fight" and that if we persevere and stick to it we will win in the end. In futures trading these notions are completely wrong. If you start losing a battle in the futures markets your best bet is usually to turn tail and run for cover. Unfortunately, because this kind of thinking runs counter to the way most of us have been taught to think, many traders focus on "fighting the good fight" rather than on cutting losses.

It sounds obvious, but it is important to remind yourself that once you lose all of your trading capital that's it—you are done trading futures. Your very first priority as a trader is to always do whatever you have to do in order to be able to trade again tomorrow. Anyone who trades long enough will score some big winning trades and/or enjoy some sustained winning periods. The trick is to stick around long enough to experience these trades and to minimize your losses in the meantime so that the big winning trades or winning streaks actually put you well into the black. In the final analysis, proper risk control is the key determinant in separating the winners from the losers in futures trading.

How To Avoid Mistake #3

The only way to avoid Mistake #3 is to plan carefully regarding the types of risk control needed for the type of trading that you are going to do and then to employ these controls without exception. Risk control falls into several categories. Some are inter-related but each can play a crucial role in ensuring a long trading career. Before going into details let's first define the role of risk control in futures trading.

The ultimate goal in trading futures is to make money, the more the better of course. However, the trade-off that needs to be considered is the relationship between total profitability and the volatility of the performance along the way. No matter how profitable a particular trading approach may be, if the day-to-day volatility of returns is too great there is a chance that you may stop trading too soon, due to either a lack of trading capital or a lack of emotional wherewithal.

As an example, consider a hypothetical trading method that makes 1000% one year and then loses 80% the next year and so on and so forth. The good news is that after 5 years a $10,000 account would be grow to $532,400—a phenomenal 121% average annual rate of return. That's the good news. The bad news is that between years one and two the account equity would plummet from $110,000 to $22,000 and between years three and four the account equity would fall from $242,000 to $48,400, before zooming to $532,400 in year five. How many traders would actually continue to take every trade given a roller coaster ride such as this? Estimated guess: zero.

Many traders start out saying "if I have to sit through a 30% drawdown, no problem, because I know my approach will make a lot of money in the end." Unfortunately, about 25% into that 30% drawdown about 90% of such traders decide they can't take it any more and they pull the plug, thereby missing the rebound that would have made them whole again.

The long-term goal of employing any risk control technique is to help keep you in the game long enough to reap substantial profits. The short-term goals of risk control are to:

- Reduce the amount of risk you expose yourself to at any given point in time
- Minimize the amount of volatility you experience on a day-to-day basis to a level you can live with and keep trading through

If you can sleep with the level of fluctuations in your account you are far more likely to stick around for the long haul. At the same time you don't want to forego a large portion of your upside potential in the process just to achieve a smooth equity curve.

Anything that reduces the magnitude of equity drawdowns goes a long way towards keeping a trader in the game for two reasons. First, it reduces the amount of money lost at any one time, thereby reducing the risk of ruin. Secondly, it can relieve a great deal of emotional pressure for the individual trader, which in turn makes him far less likely to do something drastic in the face of a sharp drawdown. *The costliest mistakes in trading are usually made when the pain of losing money (and/or the fear of losing more money) becomes too great.* It is the number one cause of bailing out when you should be staying in, doubling up when you should be cutting back, tightening stops arbitrarily (thereby guaranteeing that they will be hit), widening stops arbitrarily (thereby guaranteeing an even bigger loss on the open trade), etc., etc.

There are several risk control methods that can make a difference in your trading. You should very carefully consider the potential benefits derived from implementing each method.

Risk Control Method #1: Diversification Among Different Markets

Section One discussed some of the considerations involved in deciding whether to specialize in one market or to trade a diversified portfolio of markets. Proper diversification can go a long way towards reducing your risk of ruin. It is a commonly known fact that some markets trade similarly while others do not. The extent to which two different markets trade similarly is referred to as their "correlation." A statistical function known as the "correlation coefficient" can tell you how closely the price fluctuations of two markets mirror one another. Two markets that trade exactly the same would have a correlation coefficient of 1. On the other end of the spectrum, two markets that trade exactly the opposite would have a correlation coefficient of -1. Markets whose price movements have no correlation whatsoever would have a correlation coefficient of 0. A lack of correlation between markets offers an opportunity for astute traders to minimize the fluctuations of the equity in their account. Let's illustrate this by looking at two different portfolios.

Consider a portfolio trading T-Bonds, 10-Year T-Notes and 5-Year T-Notes using the same approach. Each of these contracts fluctuate based upon changes in interest rates. These contracts will generally rise or fall together with the main difference being the magnitude of their price movement. If you are trading them all using the same approach it is likely that at times you will be long all three contracts or short all three contracts. If interest rates are generally rising, each of these contracts will likely fall in price. If interest rates are falling, each of these contracts will likely rise in price. As a result, when you are on the right side of the market you will certainly score some big gains. However, if you are long all three contracts and interest rates spike higher you will likely take a significant hit. You may achieve good profits trading this portfolio, but in terms of risk control the thing to recognize is that you will almost certainly experience some sharp swings in account equity. If these swings are more than you can handle you may be forced to stop trading before reaping the full benefit of your approach.

Now consider an account trading a portfolio of T-Bonds, Natural Gas and the Japanese Yen. These markets fluctuate based on different variables. If you are trading them all using the same approach there is no inherent reason to expect them to trade in a similar manner. At times they may all rise or fall in unison, but more often than not they will be rising and falling independently from one another. Also, there may be periods when two of the three markets will be trading in a narrow range and offering few profitable trends. At the same time the third market may be trending strongly, thereby giving a trader the opportunity to make enough money trading that contract to offset his losses in the other two contracts.

The equity curves for these two portfolios using a particular system are shown in Figures 3-1 and 3-2. Note that the portfolio trading just the three interest rate contracts actually made more money over a four and a quarter year test period than the diversified portfolio. In retrospect, a person could say that this

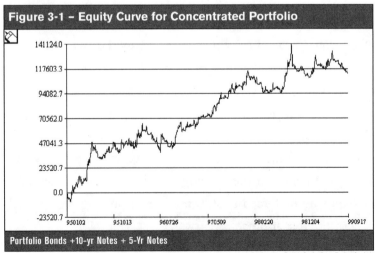

Figure 3-1 – Equity Curve for Concentrated Portfolio

Portfolio Bonds +10-yr Notes + 5-Yr Notes

Courtesy: Futures Pro by Essex Trading Co., Ltd.

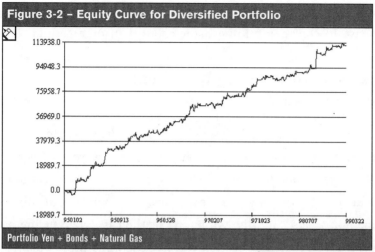

Figure 3-2 – Equity Curve for Diversified Portfolio

Portfolio Yen + Bonds + Natural Gas

Courtesy: Futures Pro by Essex Trading Co., Ltd.

was the "better" portfolio because it made more money. But take a close look at the relative choppiness of these two equity curves. Whereas the interest rate only portfolio had a number of sharp drawdowns and some drawn out flat periods, the diversified portfolio for the most part crept steadily higher throughout. Most traders would have a far easier time sticking to a trading program trading the diversified portfolio in this example, even though it earned less profits.

Risk Control Method #2: Diversification Among Trading Time Frames and Methods

In Section One we discussed the importance of determining the type of trading style (trend-following, counter-trend, etc.) and trading time frame (day trading, short-term trading, long-term trading, etc.) that are best for you. Generally, when starting out it is best to settle on one type of trading approach and to focus your efforts there. As traders progress and as their account equity grows, it makes a great deal of sense to consider trading using more than one method. Be aware that you need to have a certain level of experience and expertise in order to apply this approach, since the complexity level rises also.

The primary purpose of using multiple trading methods is to attempt to smooth out the equity fluctuations in your account. What you hope to accomplish is to apply a second method which will, in highly technical terms, "zig" while your other method "zags." Ideally, while one method is experiencing a drawdown, the other method will be generating profits to offset all or at least part of those losses.

The first step is to develop a second trading method that has a realistic probability of making money in the long run in its own right. There is no point in diversifying into a method that is going to be a drain on your trading capital simply for the sake of diversification.

To understand the potential benefits of trading in different time frames, consider the following example of a trader using both a short-term trend-following method and a long-term trend-following method to trade two contracts of each market in a diversified portfolio. Each system uses some method to identify the current market "trend." However, one system is looking at the short-term trend while the other is looking at the long-term trend. For example, one system might use a 10-day moving average of prices to identify the trend and the other system may use a 100-day moving average. At times the two systems will be "in sync." However, because the two systems are looking at the same market in two different ways, at other times one method will say the trend is "up" and the other system will say the trend is "down," or perhaps "neutral." So if the trader trades one contract of a given market based on each system, the possibilities are as follows:

Short-Term Trend	Long-Term Trend	Net Position
UP	UP	Long 2
UP	NEUTRAL	Long 1
UP	DOWN	Flat
NEUTRAL	UP	Long 1
NEUTRAL	NEUTRAL	Flat
NEUTRAL	DOWN	Short 1
DOWN	UP	Flat
DOWN	NEUTRAL	Short 1
DOWN	DOWN	Short 2

Note the effect of various market conditions on the positions held by this trader. The best situation for a trend-follower is for a strong trend to develop—no surprise there. If the short-term and long-term trends are both up or both down, the trader will have his maximum long or short position of long two or short two contracts. Under any other circumstance this trader will have either a reduced position, long one or short one, or no position at all. If the two trends are not "in sync," or if they are both neutral, the trader will have no position, i.e. no exposure in the market place. This makes perfect intuitive sense. If the trends are not in sync or if both are neutral, why would a trend-follower want a large exposure in the market place anyway?

This is only one example of how trading time frames and methods can be combined. Other examples might bc to combine a trend-following approach with a counter-trend approach, or a technical approach with a fundamental approach, etc. Assuming both approaches have positive expectations, the combined equity curve may be far less volatile than either one would be if traded separately.

Risk Control Method #3: Proper Account Sizing

This topic was discussed in great detail in Section Two. Nevertheless, because it is such an important topic it warrants another mention here. Drawdowns are the bane of futures traders. When you are making money everything is fine. It is when losses start to mount that doubt creeps in. The longer a drawdown lasts and the deeper it cuts into your equity the more painful it becomes. A trader starts to think "I wonder when I'll get back to a new equity high, or even if I'll get back up to a new equity high." It's like inadvertently getting on the down elevator in a skyrise; you don't know how long it will be before you get back to the floor you were just on.

Drawdowns are never easy to deal with. However, if you experience a drawdown that is within the realm of what you had expected going in, it is a far different situation to deal with emotionally than if you figured you would never experience anything worse than a 15% drawdown and now you are 30% in the hole. Or even worse, if you really had no idea what to expect in terms of drawdowns when you started out, and you suddenly find yourself deep in the hole. Under such circumstances it can become almost impossible to maintain confidence in your approach.

Following the steps in Section Two can give you some idea as to what you can realistically expect from your trading approach, both in terms of profitability and drawdown as a percentage of your trading capital. *By properly sizing your trading account you take an important step toward minimizing your risk even before you make the first trade.*

Risk Control Method #4: Margin-to-Equity Ratio

As discussed in detail in Section Two, one of the keys to long-term success is to develop a portfolio which is "right" for the amount of capital that you have in your account. If you trade "too small" you forego the opportunity to make money that you could make. If you trade "too big" you run the risk of experiencing sharp and occasionally painful drawdowns in your account equity, which may cause you to stop trading prematurely. This not only eliminates the opportunity to make money it also eliminates the opportunity to recoup your losses. If you trade "way too big" for your account size you run the risk of "tapping out."

While the discussion in Section Two was fairly detailed, there is a simple rule-of-thumb measure that can tell you how heavy you have your foot on the gas. This measure is referred to as the margin-to-equity ratio. To calculate this ratio simply add up the initial margin requirements for all of the positions in your portfolio. Then divide this total by the equity in your trading account to arrive at your margin-to-equity ratio. Let's look at a simple example.

Trader A has a $30,000 trading account and at any point in time may have positions in T-Bonds, Soybeans, Crude Oil and Japanese Yen. Let's also assume that the initial margin requirements for each market are as follows:

T-Bonds	**$2700**
Soybeans	**$750**
Crude Oil	**$1400**
Japanese Yen	**$2650**

If we add up these initial margin requirements we get a total of $7,500. In other words, if this trader were long or short one contract of each of these markets at the same time, his brokerage firm would require him to hold a bare minimum of $7,500 in his account. If we divide $7,500 by the $30,000 that he actually has in his account, we get a ratio of 25%. So this trader's margin-to-equity ratio is 25%. This value can and will change over time. Clearly, as the equity in his account rises or falls this value will change. Also, margin requirements that are set by the exchanges can and do change from time to time based on the fluctuations of individual markets. Finally, as the number of positions you hold rises, your margin-to-equity ratio rises, and as the number of positions you hold declines, your margin-to-equity ratio declines.

The obvious question is "what is the right margin-to-equity ratio to maintain?" If your only goal is to maximize your profitability there seemingly is no reason to limit your margin-to-equity ratio. However, the other side of the coin is risk exposure. While the margin-to-equity ratio does not measure your actual dollar risk, it does give you a quick and easy way to get a handle on the relative level of exposure you have in the market place at any given point in time. In other words, if your margin-to-equity ratio is 10%, clearly you have less exposure than if it were 30%. The ultimate goal is to maximize your profitability while minimizing your exposure to risk. If Investor A and Investor B both make 20% a year, but Investor A uses an average margin-to-equity ratio of 10% while Investor B uses an average margin-to-equity ratio of 30%, clearly Investor A is the more efficient trader as well as the one less likely to run into trouble along the way.

As far as what is the "right" margin-to-equity ratio, for this there is no absolute right or wrong answer. The general rule-of-thumb regarding a prudent maximum margin-to-equity ratio is 30%. In other words, most traders would be well advised to maintain a margin-to-equity ratio below 30%. Trading with a margin-to-equity ratio greater than 30% should be considered an "aggressive" approach to trading futures.

Risk Control Method #5: Stop-Loss Orders

Stop-loss orders are an important topic when it comes to futures trading. A stop-loss order is an order that you place with your broker to exit an open position if it reaches or exceeds a certain price. This is often referred to as a money-management stop. The purpose of a money-management stop is to attempt to limit your loss on each individual trade to a certain maximum amount.

There are several schools of thought regarding the use of stop-loss orders. Some say you should always use a stop-loss order and have it placed in the market as an open order. Some say you should use mental stops, meaning that you do not actually place the order to exit a losing trade until the market you are trading nears the stop price you had in mind. The third camp says that stop-loss orders should not be used at all, because they either interfere with the system you are using or because markets have a way of "running" stops, thereby stopping out a lot of traders just before the market goes back the other way. So which approach makes the most sense and which is the most likely to help generate the best results in the long run? Before attempting to answer this question, let's define exactly what a stop-loss order is, how it works, and the implications of using or not using stops.

Placing a Stop-Loss Order In the Market Place

Let's say you have a $20,000 trading account and have decided to risk no more than 5% of your trading capital on any single trade. You turn bullish on Soybeans and buy one contract of November Soybeans at a price of $5.00/ bushel. In an attempt to limit your risk on this trade to 5% of your trading account you decide to place a stop-loss order with your broker. 5% of $20,000 is $1,000. Soybeans trade for $50 a cent. So you can risk a $0.20 move against you. You then call your broker and place an open order (meaning it will remain in the market place until it is either filled or canceled by you) to sell one November Soybean contract at \$4.80/bushel. If Soybeans trade at or below \$4.80/bushel, your order will become a market order, meaning you will sell one contract at the current market price.

This brings up an important point. You should be aware that placing a stop-loss order at \$4.80 in this example in no way guarantees that your loss will be limited to \$1,000. Soybeans can move up or down as much as \$0.30 a day at which point it has made a "limit" move. If it rises \$0.30 from yesterday's close it cannot trade any higher. If no one is willing to sell a contract the market will remain locked at that price in what is known as a "lock limit" move. So in our example, it is possible for Soybeans to open lock limit down at \$4.70, thereby triggering your stop. However, if prices remain lock limit down (i.e. there are no buyers willing to step up) your order would not get filled and you would be sitting with a \$1,500 loss, even though you did not want to risk more than \$1,000.

Not all markets have "limits." As discussed in Section Two, this is something of a mixed blessing. If you are trading a market that does not have any daily limit then you don't need to worry about a lock limit move against you. On the other hand, there is also no real limit as to how far a market can move against you on any given day.

One disadvantage to placing an open stop order in the market place is the phenomenon that you are certain to experience if you do so. The market you are trading just seems to know where your stop is and trades to or just beyond that price just long enough to stop you out, before merrily resuming the trend that you had anticipated in the first place. If you place open stop-loss orders in the market you had better just get used to this cruel twist of Murphy's Law because it is not an uncommon occurrence.

One other complaint about stop-loss orders espoused by those who say stops should not be used is that they can interfere with the system you are using to trade. For example, say you develop a method for identifying the trend of T-Bond futures. It gives a buy signal so you buy one T-Bond contract. You also place a stop-loss order in the market place. The tricky situation that arises is when your stop-loss price is hit but your system is still bullish. Suddenly, even though you should be long in the market according to your system, you are now flat because your stop-loss order got filled. What to do, what to do?

Despite these potential negatives, placing stop-loss orders in the market does offer one significant benefit. Before discussing that benefit, let's consider the implications of using mental stops or no stops at all.

Using Mental Stops

Using a mental stop means getting into a trade, identifying a price at which you would like to exit in order to cut your loss and then waiting for the market to hit or at least get close to that price before actually placing your order in the market place. Another approach is to wait for a certain set of exit criteria to be met and then entering an order to exit the trade at that time. Mental stops are popular with traders who used to place open stop-loss orders but got sick of seeing their stops get hit just before the expected trend resumed. This type of stop is also used by large traders who don't want an open order to buy 100 T-Bond contracts sitting in the market place for fear that someone might get wind of it and "run their stop."

While mental stops can at times allow you to avoid "whip-saws," they do have one serious and (for many traders) potentially deadly fault. Consider the situation you put yourself in when you decide to use a mental stop. What you are saying is that "at the worst possible moment—when the pain of losing money on a given trade becomes too great—I will absolutely, positively pick up the phone, call my broker and place an order to stop myself out." Many traders feel that they are up to this challenge. And many traders are up to this challenge, except for that one time when they just know they are right, that the market is going to reverse at any moment, and that if they just wait a little bit longer and give the market just a little more room, then they won't have to suffer a big loss and everything will turn out OK.

The problem with putting yourself in this situation is that the scenario just described is exactly how a lot of losing traders go belly up (including losing traders who were winning traders as little as one trade prior). That one bad trade, when they just could not pull the trigger, does them in. If you have never witnessed this happen to someone, just picture standing next to your best friend while his or her house burns down and then you will get the idea. Mental stops, while perfectly logical and at times highly effective, are an invitation to disaster.

Not Using Stop-Loss Orders At All

The third camp regarding stops advocates not using stop-loss orders at all, primarily because they can interfere with the system being used to trade. At a certain level this thinking makes a great deal of sense. The underlying principle is simply this: if you have a winning system without stop-loss orders, why bother messing it up by getting yourself stopped out of trades that might otherwise end up winners? Just let the system do its thing. Unfortunately, this "certain level" is the theoretical level. And *you will find in futures trading that at times there is a chasm a mile wide between theory and reality*. This difference becomes most apparent when you actually start trading and get into a position but it starts to go horribly against you, leaving you with two choices:

a) Stick with it no matter how bad it gets because
   "my system will be profitable in the long run"

b) Run like hell

The second choice goes against the way most people think. We are raised to persevere and to fight until the end. However, when engaging in an endeavor that exposes you to unlimited risk, the very qualities that may earn you admiration in other areas of life can cost you large sums of money. The long-term goal in futures trading is to win the war, not each individual battle.

The One Important Benefit of Stop-Loss Orders

Earlier we discussed the negatives associated with placing open stop-loss orders in the market place. Despite these negatives, this approach offers one significant advantage over other alternatives. Before unveiling that advantage let's first define what a stop-loss order is intended/and not intended to accomplish.

The purpose of a stop-loss order is not to enhance the performance of your system. Likewise, the purpose of a stop-loss order is not directly to increase the profitability of your trading. The purpose of a stop-loss order is to hopefully minimize your losses on any bad trade enough so that you can still come back to trade again tomorrow. Nothing more, nothing less. A wise old trader once said it best when he stated "the purpose of a stop-loss order is to save your sorry assets."

The way to make money trading futures is to stick around long enough to earn enough profits to offset all of the inevitable losses. If your approach to trading stinks, stop-loss orders won't make you a profitable trader. However, if you do have a winning approach to trading the only thing that can derail you is "that one bad trade" or that series of huge losses that knock you out. The only way to safeguard against huge losses is to use stops to protect your capital. And the only way to guarantee that your stop-loss order will be in the market when it needs to be is for your stop-loss order to indeed be there.

In case you are having trouble reading between the lines, this author advocates the use of stop-loss orders.

Summary

In any endeavor there are certain objectives that must be achieved in order to succeed. Yet before you can even think about winning you have to first put yourself in a position to win. To win a war you must advance your troops and take up land. Yet an army that refuses to ever acknowledge the order to retreat is unlikely to survive. To win in auto racing you must be the fastest driver. But a racecar driver who refuses to ever slow down is far more likely to crash than to win a race. In professional poker you need to win a lot of hands in order to make a living. However, a professional gambler who refuses to ever walk away from the table will eventually lose all of his chips.

In the end, risk control will not single handedly win the war, the race, or the game for you. Yet without proper risk control you have no hope of winning. Therefore, the only way to win the war or the race or the game is to do what must be done in order to ensure your long-term survival. And that is what risk control is all about. *Risk control is what keeps you in the game long enough to have a chance to win.*

This is true for any risky endeavor and futures trading is no exception. While cutting a loss and exiting a trade does not get you closer to your goal of making x-dollars, it does keep you from *getting further away* from that goal. The same holds true for all of the risk control measures discussed in this section. While employing these steps may not directly put money in your pocket, they do allow you to stay in the game long enough to accomplish your objectives. Conversely, *refusing to employ effective risk control measures can ensure your long-term failure.*

MISTAKE #4
Lack of Discipline

What is Mistake #4

Let's say you are new to futures trading. Or let's say you have traded futures in the past without much success and have decided to start fresh with a new approach and a clean slate. And you've done it all and followed every step.

You have:

- Determined how much money you can truly afford to risk

- Opened a brokerage account with that amount of cash

- Settled on a diversified portfolio of markets

- Developed a trading system in which you have complete confidence

- Developed specific, unambiguous entry and exit criteria

- Back-tested your system and have generated good hypothetical results

- Walked your system forward, paper traded it over new data and have generated good results

- Sized your account so that you reasonably expect no more than a 25% drawdown

- Built in risk controls including stop-loss orders to minimize your risk

You're as ready as you can be. With high hopes and great anticipation you place an order to enter your first trade. So what happens next? Well, if you are like many traders the first three trades you make will be losses. After the first loss, you'll say "no big deal; it's part of trading." After the second loss you'll think "I wonder if I'm doing something wrong." After the third loss you'll tell yourself "something's wrong, and I need to regroup." You will have no idea why your system has suddenly fallen apart. So you decide to go flat and skip the next signal, a buy signal. Two days later the market that you should be long explodes to the upside leaving you in the dust. You tell yourself "it's too late to jump on board now, so I'll just wait for the next trade," relieved at least that your confidence in your system has been restored. So you wait for the next signal from your system. And you wait and you wait and you wait. And in the meantime that market continues to tack on gains virtually every day. Your system is doing great, but you on the other hand are not doing so well. You start mentally adding the money that you *should* have made on this trade to your account and say "I should have this much in my account now." But every day your account balance remains the same, while that market just keeps rising higher and higher. By the time you enter the next trade you have a missed a $5,000 winner. And the next trade is another loser.

If you are one of the lucky ones, at this point your loss is relatively small, you conclude that you are in over your head, and you decide that enough is enough. You close your account and walk away, joining that fateful 90%. For the rest of your life whenever the topic of futures trading comes up you step forward like a veteran with a purple heart and tell your "war story:" "yeah, I traded futures, listen to me kid......."

Or maybe you don't quit so easily. If you are one of the unlucky ones, you keep trading, suffer more indignities at the hands of the futures markets, and lose even more money before your account is finally laid to rest. And so it goes for 90% of the people who enter the exciting world of commodities speculation.

Given all of the potential pitfalls that we have discussed so far it is easy to understand why the person who decides to "take a shot" and is completely unprepared fails at futures trading. But what about the trader in this example? He was completely prepared both financially and emotionally to do what was necessary to succeed and still he failed. Why does this happen to so many traders sincerely dedicated to "making it work?" In most cases it is because although they were very well prepared when they began their new trading program, somewhere along the way they failed to do what was needed. They failed to have the discipline to pull the trigger (or to not pull the trigger as the case may be), and they either suffered a loss or missed a huge profit. With many traders this can cause an emotional "domino effect" where the trader's primary focus is no longer on following his plan to achieve his long-term objectives. Instead, his primary objective becomes getting back at the markets for causing him to lose money or for taking off without him. Or maybe his objective is simply to get back to "break even" before walking away. Becoming bent on getting even is a perfectly natural response to a kick in the teeth. Unfortunately, it is also a sure-fire way to fail as a futures trader.

A lack of discipline is defined as failing to do what you should do in a given circumstance. There is probably not a trader alive, successful or otherwise, who has never suffered because of his or her own lack of discipline at some critical moment. What separates those who make money in the long run from the other 90% is: • The financial and emotional capabilities to survive a breach in discipline. • The willingness to learn from mistakes and to never repeat a mistake already made. A lack of discipline in futures trading is always a mistake. This is true even if your lack of discipline actually saves you money by skipping a trade or exiting early, or if it allows you to capture a windfall profit by taking a trade against your approach, doubling up on a losing trade or holding on after your trading method tells you to exit. Imagine, you fail to follow your plan and you come out ahead. This leaves you ahead financially for the moment but consider where this leaves you psychologically: "I broke my own rules and made some money." All is well and good in the short run but what happens the next time a critical juncture is reached? Do you trust the approach that you spent so much time developing and refining (and which in the back of your mind "failed" you the last time around, while you, Mr. Supertrader, instinctively knew it was going to fail so you heroically took matters into your own hands and won the day), or your own "gut" instincts?

The most cruel paradox in futures trading is that a trader's short-term successes can plant the seeds of his long-term failure. Believe it or not, one of the worst things that can happen to a first time trader is to have great success right off the bat. In the long run you may actually be better off if you struggle a little at the outset, develop some respect for the markets and weather some early mistakes, than if your first three trades are big winners and you decide you've got "the touch."

Why Do Traders Make Mistake #4

A lack of discipline in trading is almost always the result of one or more of the three great obstacles to trading success:

- Fear

- Greed

- Ego

Every time a trader makes a decision regarding any element of his trading he is subject to the effects of fear, greed and ego. This does not imply that we all need hours of serious therapy. It is simply human nature taking over. We all want to make money (thus we feel greed) and we don't want to lose money (thus we feel fear). Cutting a loss is extremely tough on the ego. Once you cut a loss on a trade there is no chance to recoup that loss without entering into an entirely new trade. This explains why cutting a loss is often such a difficult thing to do. How many people enjoy going around and voluntarily admitting mistakes, especially ones that cost them money? Not very many. It simply goes against human nature. Yet when trading futures it is often exactly the right thing to do.

These emotions are at times so powerful that they can cause you to do all kinds of foolish things:

- You bail out of a trade prematurely with a small loss simply because you don't want to risk a bigger loss (fear/ego).

- You stop trading altogether during a drawdown— right before things turn around (fear).

- You take a profit prematurely because you don't want to give it back, thereby missing a big profit (greed).

- You double up or increase your position size in an effort to get back to break-even or in an effort to "make a killing" (greed).

This list goes on and on ad infinitum.

How To Avoid Mistake #4

Of the four biggest mistakes in futures trading, a lack of discipline is the most difficult mistake to avoid. The other mistakes detailed in this book can all be dealt with before you start a trading program. You can lay out every step of your trading program down to the last detail. But then you must pull the trigger. That is when Mistake #4 comes into play. As a result, the opportunities to make this mistake are limitless.

A lack of discipline occurs while you are in the line of fire. Picture a new soldier who goes to military school, boot camp and engages in other extensive training. Then suddenly he finds himself in live combat for the first time with somebody shooting real bullets at him. Now consider an individual new to futures trading. He has planned everything and knows exactly what needs to be done in order to ensure his long term survival. Then he suddenly finds himself in a difficult situation, with real money—his money—on the line. How people react in difficult situations cannot be known until that time arrives. Hopefully their planning and preparation will allow them to overcome any psychological obstacles. But you never know for sure how they will react until the moment of truth arrives.

Just telling yourself to put fear and greed and ego aside won't do the trick. You must identify the points within your own trading plan where you will most likely confront these obstacles and make plans to avoid their negative effects. For example, if your approach requires you to interpret chart patterns, you need to define your rules very carefully to remove as much subjectivity as possible. If you do not, you may find yourself interpreting the same pattern differently at times. If your trading has not been going well lately it may be easy to find some perfectly justifiable reason not to take the next trade. Likewise, if you are planning to use mental stops you must prepare yourself to always follow through and to place orders as needed. If you fail to do so, then one bad trade can do you in.

Overcoming The IQ Obstacle

Peter is at the Gates of Heaven. A long line of souls are waiting to enter. Peter is frantic. "Quick," says Peter to the first in line, "what is your IQ?" "Why, my IQ is 210," replies the first soul. "No, no, get out of line!" yells Peter. "You, what's your IQ?" he asks the next soul. "175" is the reply. "No, that's no good!" cries Peter as he continues to works his way down the line. "150," "130," "110" come the replies. But still Peter is frantic. Finally he reaches a poor soul whose reply to Peter's question is "my IQ is 75." "Oh, Thank God!" cries Peter. "Now quick, tell me, where did November Soybeans close today?"

This story gets passed along from one self-deprecating futures trader to another and everyone has a good laugh. The implication is that all futures traders are dimly lit. This is certainly not the case. However, there is one element of truth to this story that needs to be addressed: believe it or not, intelligence can be an obstacle to trading success. This is not to say that intelligent people cannot be and are not successful in the area of futures trading. All it means is that their intelligence can work against them at times. How so you may ask? Well, one thing that intelligent people do is to analyze things more deeply than others. In futures trading such a propensity can be a very dangerous thing.

Futures markets do all kinds of unpredictable things. They go up when everyone thinks they are going to go down. They go down when everyone thinks they are going to go up. They may have no reaction at all to a major piece of fundamental news. They may have a big reaction to a seemingly trivial piece of news, etc. None of which makes the least bit of sense. And therein lies the rub. Intelligent people like things to "make sense" to them. If something does not make sense to them then it needs to be analyzed so that an understanding can be gained. In futures trading trying to understand exactly *why* something is happening can be a costly exercise in futility.

Consider the following scenario. A person with an IQ of 200 is short T-Bond futures because he expects the next unemployment report to show a sharp decline in unemployment, indicating a stronger than expected economy. He believes that such news will cause interest rates to rise and T-Bond futures to plummet. He figures he will risk $1000 per contract using a mental stop. On Friday morning the unemployment report comes out and it is exactly what he had expected. The numbers are sharply lower. Our trader has nailed it right on the money. But there is one small problem. T-Bond futures have started to rally sharply. How can this be? Apparently a lot of other traders had been anticipating the same number and had also been selling short in recent days. Now that the bad news is out of the way and all the sellers have already sold, the buyers take charge and T-Bonds inexplicably shoot higher. Within two minutes of the report's release our trader is sitting with an $1,200 loss. And here is where intelligence becomes an obstacle.

The natural thing to do is to immediately begin mentally processing "why" this has happened. "I got it exactly right. How can I be losing money? What's going on here?" our trader might ask himself. And he will begin trying to make sense of a market that is rallying in the face of incontrovertibly bearish news. All the while his losses mount. By the time he finally pulls the trigger he has lost over $1,600 a contract. What should he have done? When he entered the trade he told himself he would risk no more than $1,000. Right after the news came out he was down $1,200. What he should have done was cut his loss immediately at that exact moment as he had planned to when he entered the trade. But because his thought processes forced him to try to make sense of things first he did not pull the trigger when he needed to. This type of scenario plays out all the time, which leads to the next bit of advice.

A Word of Advice: Don't Think, React

Here is another example of how futures trading is quite different from everything else in life. In every other endeavor we are taught to think first, then react. In futures trading—with a caveat to follow—you are often far better off reacting first and then thinking later. The caveat is this: this is only true if you have developed and are executing a well thought out trading plan. If you decide that you will exit a particular trade if a certain set of criteria is met, then that is exactly what you need to do. *The specific chain of events that caused your exit criteria to be met are completely irrelevant.* While they can be analyzed after the fact for information that may help in the future, they cannot be allowed to convince you to do one thing when you know you should be doing something else.

At the most base level consider a floor trader who typically scalps the market trying to make two or three ticks per trade. He is long 30 T-Bond contracts when a huge wave of sell orders hits the trading floor. He has two potential courses of action:

a) Stand around and try to figure out "why" a wave of selling is occurring

b) Start hitting bids instantly to exit his long positions

If he is a good floor trader and if he wants to survive, he will choose b. In other words, he needs to react immediately. Every second he spends analyzing the situation costs him money.

If a situation arises for which you have already determined exactly what you should do in case of just such an event, react and do it. Don't think (whoever thought you'd hear that kind of advice?). If a situation arises for which you have not prepared, and you have no idea how to react, then think in terms of risk control. Ask yourself, "what are my choices and which one is the least likely to result in a huge loss?" Then do that.

Avoid Simple Traps

There once was a trader who adopted a trend-following, position trading approach and was quite successful. His approach was to generate a trading order for the next day after the close of trading each day and to always follow his system. Although he was not a day trader, he obtained real-time quotes from his data vendor, ostensibly to keep better track of his successes. One day, in the midst of a strong intermediate-term rally, he was long four contracts of Lumber with an order to sell short at 4080. In the opening minutes of trading his order was hit and he was reversed into a short position. A few minutes after that a report came out that caused Lumber to soar higher by almost its full daily limit. Suddenly this trader was down $3,712 on four contracts in just a matter of minutes. Completely distraught he tried to figure out what to do. Should he cover his short position immediately? Should he hold on? What is the proper course of action? Fearing that the market would "lock" limit higher, he covered his short position and went flat. Would it surprise you to learn that by the end of the day, Lumber closed back down exactly at the price at which he had shorted it earlier that day? The next day Lumber opened sharply lower and just kept sinking. Instead of losing a little on the first day and holding a profitable short position the next, our trader suffered a loss of $3,712 and could not bring himself to get back into the short position, thereby missing out on a subsequent $10,240 profit. His momentary lack of discipline cost him $13,952. Ouch!

Where did this trader go wrong? Two things come to mind. First off, if you have made the decision not to be a day trader, then live quotes can be a very dangerous thing. To the undisciplined trader a quote machine can be the equivalent of a slot machine. You see the opportunities flashing before your eyes and you feel compelled to play.

Also, based on his trading approach, by all rights the trader in this example should not even have been aware of Lumber's intraday gyrations. Had he been off reading a good book instead of staring at his quote screen he would not only have saved himself a considerable sum of money, but also all of the emotional angst that went with watching the market move sharply against him, arbitrarily deciding to bail out, and then watching the market move back in the right direction without him being on board.

The second error this trader made was in failing to adhere to his approach. His system told him to be short, but he succumbed to fear and stopped himself out at the point of maximum pain. *The markets do not know that you are long or short and certainly do not move in a particular way simply to inflict pain upon you personally. It just seems that way sometimes.*

One key to longevity is to know the following: The markets will frustrate you and inflict pain upon you from time to time. This is simply a fact of trading life. *The trick is to not frustrate nor inflict pain upon yourself.* The markets are going to do whatever they are going to do and there is no way that you can control them. The only thing you can control is your reaction to market events. Your best bet for doing so is to have a well thought out plan and to follow it precisely. *If you succumb to fear or greed or ego you become your own worst enemy.* Knowing yourself as well as you do, do you really want you as your worst enemy?

The Cure for "Woulda, Shoulda, Coulda": Points A,B,C, and D

Because there is always so much room for improvement between what you could have made and what you did make it is very easy for traders to spend a lot of time fixating on what might have been, the dreaded "woulda, shoulda, coulda" syndrome. "If only I had gotten in sooner (or later) and exited sooner (or later). If only this, if only that....." This is a difficult malady to avoid, particularly because it can affect you even if you are making money. Interestingly, as much as traders hate losing money, quite possibly the single most frustrating experience in futures trading is to close a trade with a profit and then have the market explode causing you to miss out on a much larger profit than the one you took. The only way to avoid the "woulda, shoulda, coulda" syndrome is, when trading, to *focus solely on the action of the market from the time you enter the trade until the time you exit the trade*. For the sake of your own sanity, what happened before you entered and after you exited the trade should be ignored (for now).

Traders often focus their attention in the wrong places. Consider an undisciplined trader who enters a long position after a market has already experienced a sharp advance. Instead of focusing on the trade itself and being thankful he climbed aboard at all, this trader will constantly admonish himself, sighing "I should have gotten in sooner!" After the trader exits this trade with a nice profit the market keeps rallying without our trader on board. He now beats himself with "I should have stayed in longer!" And the next time he finds himself in a similar situation he does everything just the opposite way. He jumps in too soon and the market tanks. He stubbornly continues to hold on because he doesn't want to miss "the big rally," which this time around never comes.

The antidote to the dreaded "woulda, shoulda, coulda" syndrome is twofold:

- The first part is to understand the psychological significance of Points A, B, C, and D.
- The second part is to separate the act of trading from the act of trading system development.

What are Points A, B, C, and D?

- Point A to Point B is what happens to the market before you get into the trade.

- Point B to Point C is what happens to the market while you are in the trade.

- Point C to Point D is what happens to the market after you exit the trade.

From a trading standpoint the thing to remember is this:

- *The ONLY thing that really matters is what happens between Point B and Point C.*

- *Point A to Point B (what happens before you enter the trade) is irrelevant.*

- *Point C to Point D (what happens after you exit the trade) is irrelevant.*

Adopting this mindset can relieve a trader of a tremendous amount of excess emotional baggage. But this mindset also begs several key questions. "Shouldn't I be trying to improve my system?" "Doesn't it make sense to look at ways to enter and exit trades more efficiently?" "And if so, by ignoring Point A to Point B and Point C to Point D aren't I ignoring possibly useful information that might improve my trading results on future trades?" The answers to these questions are "yes," "yes" and "yes." However, *the time to address these questions is NOT when you are in the middle of a trade.* The time to focus on these questions is when you are focusing your efforts on developing a trading approach or enhancing your current approach, in other words, when the markets are closed and your mind is clear. This leads us to another cause of lack of discipline know as "system tinkering."

System Development Versus System "Tinkering"

Using an objective, systematic approach to trading offers several benefits to a trader. He can do his best thinking "up front," build all of his knowledge and experience into a system and then let the system generate the trading signals. This in turn removes the psychological burden of having to make a lot of trading decisions while standing in the line of fire. It also can remove ego from the trading process, thereby eliminating one of the three primary causes of Mistake #4. If a particular trade loses money, it can be blamed on the system and the trader does not need to blame himself.

One pitfall that snares a lot of systematic traders is the urge to constantly "tinker" with their trading system. One problem with developing a trading system is that it never quite feels like it's "done." No matter how good a given system performs, the ambitious trader can't help but to think that there must be some way to alter it to improve performance ("...maybe if I lengthened this oscillator or shortened this moving average..."). In the minds of most system traders the best trading system is the one you haven't developed yet. Once a system is "done" it never looks quite as good as it might have. This is what causes traders to tinker.

The danger is that if you are constantly tinkering with your existing system, then you may never truly develop the confidence in it that you need to have in order to stick with it when the going gets tough. If you are tinkering with your system while you are trading, it is likely that you will start changing the rules or adding new rules as you go to match your most recent experience. If you exited the last trade too soon you may find yourself adding another rule to your system to hold trades longer (which may be exactly the wrong thing to do the next time around). If your last four trades were losers in quick succession you may find yourself adding a rule designed to "filter" trades and thereby avoid some whipsaws. While well intentioned and perfectly logical, this may cause you to miss the next big winner altogether. Over time your system starts to look like a house that started out as a two bedroom shanty. Then a garage was added, then a family room, then an upstairs, etc., etc. In other words, it ends up not even resembling its original form. There is nothing wrong with adjusting a trading system. There is, however, a time and a place for everything.

The best advice is to designate a specific time—whether it is once a month, once a quarter, or whatever—at which time you will sit down and analyze all aspects of your system to determine if you have learned anything since the last time that you can use to add value to your current approach. This is when you want to analyze Point A to B and Point C to D for previous trades to determine if you can improve the efficiency of your entries and exits. Doing so in this manner allows you to delve into your system as deeply as you want without the emotional attachment that might otherwise cloud your judgment if you were making a change based solely on your last trade.

The proper approach in order to avoid system tinkering is to:

- Develop the best system that you can given your current knowledge base and experience.

- Start trading.

- At scheduled intervals—even while you continue to trade using your original system—open up and

> analyze each part of your trading system and see if
> there is anything new that you can add or subtract
> that might add value. Approach this process with
> the attitude that "if I improve my system, great,
> but if not that's OK too."

Following these steps allows you to separate trading from
trading system development. Focusing on one task at a time
will make you better and more efficient at both.

Asking The Right Question

One thing that is very important is to ask the "right" question. This is an extremely simple concept but some traders are
doomed to failure because they only look at things one way
and therefore don't examine all of the possible outcomes in a
given situation. When you are considering entering a given
trade there are two primary questions to be asked and
answered. The first question is "what is the likelihood that
the market will move in the right direction?" The second
question is "what will I do if the market moves against me?"
The problem is that traders often focus too much attention on
the first question and not enough on the second.

Your answer to the first question represents your theory
regarding what you think is likely to happen next in the market. Your answer to the second question represents your fail-
safe plan should disaster strike. *In the long run what will make
the biggest difference in your success or failure is not your prediction about what is going to happen in each situation, but how
you react when things don't go the way you expect them to.* This
is a case of theory versus reality. In theory, you may feel,

based upon your analysis, that your risk on a given trade is low. That's all well and good, but what if the reality of the situation turns out to be different? Are you prepared to deal with that situation? This is what asking the right question is all about.

When a trader considers buying a contract of Soybeans he asks the question "will it go down?" If he enters the trade then obviously he believes the answer is "no" or he wouldn't put the trade on in the first place. However, answering this question provides a trader with nothing more than the rationalization for entering into and holding onto the trade. No matter how certain he is that his analysis is correct, statistically the odds remain 50/50 that the market will rise after he buys. Once he puts the trade on all the brilliant analysis in the world isn't going to help him one bit. The only thing that matters from that point forward is "does he make money or does he lose money?" Regardless of what a trader thinks is going to happen and why, the market will move however it sees fit.

By putting all of their focus on the first question traders can fall into the trap of false confidence, which can cause them to not bother answering the "right" question which is "what will I do if the market goes the wrong way?" A trader may reassure himself by saying "I'm so sure the market is going up that I'm not worried about the downside" (which is tantamount to whistling past the graveyard). Try to argue with this trader by asking him "but what will you do if the market *does* go down?" and he will likely counter with a list of reasons why he doesn't think it will, as if any of them really matter.

To borrow a stock market example, a trader takes a huge position in Wal-Mart stock. When asked what he perceives his downside risk to be he replies "Nil." His reasoning? "Wal-Mart's practically got a monopoly" (whatever that means). One thing it does mean is that this trader has not asked the right question. He has answered the question "will it go down" with a reason why he believes it will not. He is also using this answer as a rationalization to not bother answering the more important question "what will I do if it does go down?" This trader could be standing on the edge of a canyon but he refuses to even acknowledge the risk in front of him.

The purpose of asking the right question is simple. In order to survive long-term, in each situation you must be prepared ahead of time to deal with the potential risks involved. Be sure to constantly ask yourself, "what is the worst case scenario and what will I do if it unfolds?" If you always have an answer to this question you have the potential to be a highly successful futures trader. On the other side of the coin, *if you find yourself reassuring yourself that, based on your analysis, you have nothing to worry about, then you DO have something to worry about.* If you have no real contingency plan for protecting yourself if you turn out to be wrong, be afraid, be very afraid. Remember, it only takes one bad trade to wipe out a lot of hard earned money. If you don't believe me, ask Victor Neiderhoffer.

Summary

One of the keys to long-term trading success is to develop an approach to trading that removes as many outside (and often irrelevant) influences as possible from the decision making process. At any given point in time there are at least a million and one reasons available to justify *not* doing what your trading method tells you to do. What a trader must do in order to succeed—and one of the things that make successful futures trading so difficult—is to ignore all one million and one reasons and do what you are supposed to do anyway. Richard Dennis referred to this as "doing the hard thing."

In one of the most successful experiments ever conducted in the area of futures trading, Richard Dennis and another trader recruited a group of individuals they dubbed the "Turtles" in the late 1970's. What they did was to bring in a group of individuals with no prior experience in trading with the goal of teaching them to be successful traders. The challenge was to find out if individuals are born great traders or whether individuals could be taught to be great traders. The Turtles collectively have enjoyed great success thanks to some of the important lessons they learned along the way. One of the things they were taught was to "do the hard thing." Some examples:

- If you get a signal to go short on the next day's open and the market gaps sharply lower the next day, the easiest thing to do is to not make the trade ("it's too late; it's already made a big move"). The hard thing to do—and the right thing to do—is to make the trade anyway.

- If you are in a long position using a mental stop and the market in question reaches your stop price but is now extremely oversold and certainly appears to be due to bounce, the easiest thing to do is to wait just a little longer before exiting the trade. The hard thing to do—and the right thing to do—is to cut your loss anyway and move on.

- Richard Dennis gave the Turtles a test and one of the questions was "Your system tells you to buy Soybeans. You find out that I (Richard Dennis) am selling short heavily in the Soybean market. What should you do?

  a) Buy anyway

  b) Sell short

  c) Wait for another signal

The easiest thing to do is to put off making the trade. The hard thing to do, and the right thing to do, is, a) buy anyway.

Second guessing a trading decision is the single most simple act in all of futures trading. It is also one of the deadliest habits in all of futures trading. If you find yourself repeatedly second guessing your trading approach and making things up as you go along, it is time to stop trading and develop a new approach.

The moral of the story: *A lack of discipline can destroy even the most talented and best prepared trader.*

CONCLUSION

Many books on trading attempt to boost traders' confidence by suggesting ways to make trading success easier to come by. And certainly most traders would prefer that trading success be "easy" to achieve. The purpose of this book, however, has been quite the opposite. One of the goals of this book has been to strip away all of the hype and hope and pretense and to lay bare the fact that success in futures trading is no easier to achieve than success in any other field. By now you have hopefully rid yourself of the notion that trading futures is going to line your pockets with "easy money." If you are to make money as a futures trader, make no mistake: you will earn it.

One primary goal of this book has been to instill the realization that there is only one person who can control your success or failure as a futures trader (as well as everything else in life for that matter). And that person is you. *In the end you are responsible for your own trading success or failure.* You now know that the futures markets, while seductive and very accommodating at times, can be cruel and unforgiving and will cause you to suffer greatly from time to time no matter how great of a trader you might end up to be. How you deal with this simple fact of reality will determine if you join the 10% of winning traders or the other 90%.

One of the most common pitfalls in futures trading is for something to go very wrong for a trader, for that trader to blame the markets rather than himself, and for a negative experience to cause a downward spiral in his trading. Working past a bad trading experience is doubly difficult because not only does it leave you emotionally feeling (lousy, angry, or frustrated, it leaves you with less money to your name. Now that really hurts. *The key is to understand and accept the simple fact that this is part of life as a trader and to not allow a bad experience to have a negative residual effect on subsequent trades.* This is easier said than done.

For example, say you are long Crude Oil, which closed yesterday at $21.60/barrel. Today you enter an order to sell short at $21.00. Crude Oil trades down to exactly $21.00 and you get reversed into a short position. Crude Oil then rallies back up to close unchanged at $21.60. For the day you lost $600 on the long side plus $600 on the short side for a total loss of $1,200. The next day you pick up the paper and the story reads "...and Crude Oil closed unchanged in dull trading." "Dull trading?" you might scream. "I lost $1,200 bucks. What's so dull about that you !@#$%!." This is but one of many possible examples, but the common result is a maddening feeling of frustration and a desperate need to "act" to somehow make things "right."

A trader is left wondering why he or she was so "unlucky." "How could I sell short at the *exact* low of the day? Why did the market single me out? I can't blame myself. I placed my stop right where my system told me to." The danger here is that a trader may suddenly feel a compelling urge to "act" in order to compensate for the bad experience just completed. *This is a mistake.*

Losing traders follow through on this urge to act. Winning traders do not. Winning traders do what they are supposed to do.

If a bad trade leaves you wanting to double up to get even or to widen your stops next time around, etc., etc., you are in danger of making a critical error. And doing so can send you down a very slippery slope. Think back to when you were a kid and you stole a cookie out of the cookie jar despite specific instructions not to do so. The first time you did it you were wracked with guilt. But wasn't it so much easier the second time around? And by the third and fourth time it was almost fun to figure out new ways to do something that you knew you should not do. This is an appropriate analogy for a futures trader.

The first time you violate your trading plan it involves a tremendous amount of angst. You know you are contemplating doing something you should not, but eventually you come up with enough reasons to "justify" (or more accurately, rationalize) violating your plan. And so you do. And you find that it's not that hard to do after all. No one questions you or tries to stop you. The trading police don't show up and haul you away. You just call your broker, place an order (or change an order or cancel an order) and the deed is done. No muss, no fuss.

And the next time you find yourself contemplating another deviation from your trading plan, you find it is "way easier" than the time before. In the short-term it couldn't be much easier. In the long-term there is one drawback: *In so doing you have stepped down the path of the 90% of futures traders who lose money.* Whatever the market did to you to cause you to act this way is not relevant. What is relevant is this: *only you can make the decision to turn around and head back toward the right path and to stay there.*

I hope that the material in this book helps you to do so.

Appendix A
Mathematical Formula for Standard Deviation

Standard Deviations

Standard deviation is simply a measure of distribution. It shows how data is clustered around the average value for a given set of data. For a given set of data, a one standard deviation move above and below the average encompasses ⅔rds of the data under consideration. A two standard deviation move above and below the average includes 96% of the data and a three standard deviation move above and below the average includes 99% of the data.

Section Two discussed measuring standard deviations of monthly returns in order to arrive at a conservative account size for a given portfolio. The following formula can be used to calculate the standard deviation of any group of data. The first step is to calculate the "average" value. The second step measures the deviations from the average to arrive at the standard deviation.

- Step 1 — Calculate the Average Value over the Number of Periods under Consideration

  This is accomplished by adding up the sum of all of the values and dividing by the number of periods:

  sum1 = 0
  For x = 1 to Number of Periods
  sum1 = sum1 + value(x)
  Next x
  average = (sum1 / Number of Periods)

- Step 2 — Calculate the Deviation from the Average for Each Value

- Step 3 — Calculate the Standard Deviation

Steps 2 and 3 are done by:

a) Subtracting each value from the average.
b) Squaring "a" (simply multiply "a" times "a").
c) Sum the value for "b" for each value.
d) Take the square root of ("c" divided by Number of Periods).

sum2 = 0
For x = 1 To Number of Periods
sum2 = sum2 + ((average, value(x) x (average, value(x))
Next x
Standard Deviation = Square Root(sum2 / Number of Periods)

Trading
Resource
Guide

❖

Tools for Success
in Futures Trading

SUGGESTED READING LIST

STRATEGIES FOR THE ELECTRONIC FUTURES TRADER,

Jake Bernstein — The electronic revolution has yanked the rug out from yesterday's floor-based futures traders, and opened the doors to all traders with a personal computer and a hunger for trading. This new book gives you all the information you need to get started and details the tools you need to control risk, while reaping profits in this fast moving market.

$39.95 ITEM C79X-10613

COMPLETE GUIDE TO ELECTRONIC FUTURES TRADING:
EVERYTHING YOU NEED TO START TRADING ONLINE,

Scott Slutsky, Darrell Jobman — In this comprehensive guide the authors of Masters of the Futures walks futures traders through everything they need for profitable online trading from order-handling systems to the critical differences between traditional and online trading.

$29.95 ITEM C79X-10616

SCHWAGER FUTURES: *FUNDAMENTAL ANALYSIS,* Jack Schwager

— The most comprehensive guide to using fundamental analysis exclusively for futures traders by the author of the run away best sellers, *Market Wizards* and *New Market Wizards*.

$65.00 ITEM C79X-2587

Master the skills for applying fundamental analysis to futures trading with this thorough practice guide.

STUDY GUIDE $30.00 ITEM C79X-2487
GET BOTH FOR $87.00 ITEM C79X-2573

JOHN MURPHY ON CHART ANALYSIS, Renowned market technician
John Murphy presents basic principles of technical and chart analysis in this easy to undertstand booklet. It's a full resource guide to industry's top tools to obtain a better understanding of what charts can do — and how they can help you grab your portion of today's trading profits. A Bridge/CRB CD-rom is included containing a full suite of charting tools allowing you to implement what you learn as you go.

$19.95 ITEM C79P1X-10593

Many of these books along with hundreds and hundreds of others are available at a discount from Traders' Library. To place an order or find out more, visit us at www.traderslibrary.com or call us at 1-800-272-2855.

DEFINITIVE GUIDE TO FUTURES TRADING, VOLUME I,

Larry Williams — He won the World Cup Championship of Futures Trading and now he reveals the winning methods he pioneered — including the accumulation/distribution method and the %R method — which revolutionized the futures industry.

$55.00 ITEM C79X-2586

DEFINITIVE GUIDE TO FUTURES TRADING, VOLUME II,

Larry Williams — includes 50 pages of Larry's personal day trading knowledge along with a money management technique giving you great odds to double your money.

$55.00 ITEM C79X-2588

GETTING STARTED IN FUTURES, *Todd Lofton* — To enjoy the

rewards of the futures market with minimal risk, this newly revised primer should be your first stop. It's the universal choice for beginning investors in the futures market.

$18.95 ITEM C79X-5692

THE NEW CRB COMMODITY YEARBOOK, *Bridge Information*

Systems — Dubbed the "bible" by market analysts and traders since 1939, the CRB Commodity Yearbook provides invaluable reverence information on 105 domestic and international commodities. It includes seasonal patterns and historical data from the past ten years, as well as pricing and trading patterns on a monthly and annual basis.

$99.95 ITEM C79X-10531

Now available on CD-rom! 30 years of historical Fundamental Data on over 100 markets in one convenient source. Similar to the annual yearbook, the CD version offers immediate access to every yearbook since 1965 using the QuickSearch feature.

$195.00 ITEM C79X-10229

MAGIC OF MOVING AVERAGES, *Scott Lowery* — After years of

exhaustive research, Lowry shows that the simple, quick and practical moving average method is an extremely provitable approach to trading in the futures market. $29.95 ITEM C79X-10219

TECHNICAL ANALYSIS OF FUTURES MARKET: *A COMPREHENSIVE GUIDE TO TRADING METHODS ETHODS AND APPLICATIONS,*
John J. Murphy — Complete guide to all aspects of technical trading. Written by the world's leading technical expert, this book details hundreds of indicators, their derivations, applications, and shortcomings.

$59.95 ITEM C79X-2366

BE A WINNER TRADING COMMODITIES,
Ralph Fessenden, Ph.D. — Here's virtually the first improvement in Scale Trading technicques in over 24 years. Step-by-step guide shows how to take advantage of powerful supply/demand forces by using scale trading methods.

$29.95 ITEM C79X-10550

NEW MARKET WIZARDS, *Jack Schwager* — Meet a new generation of market killers. These winning traders make millions, often in hours, and consistently out perform peers. Trading across a spectrum of financial markets, they use different methods but share remarkable successes. How do they do it?? How can you do it??

$39.95 ITEM C79X-2106

THE FOUR BIGGEST IN OPTIONS TRADING, *Jay Kaeppel* —
You can earn big profits in options trading by avoiding the 4 most common—and costly—mistakes the majority of traders make. The author shows you how to avoid common pitfalls option traders encounter that cause them to lose money in the long run.

$19.95 ITEM C79X-8471

Important Internet Sites

TRADERS' LIBRARY BOOKSTORE —
www.traderslibrary.com, the #1 source for trading and investment books, videos, and related products.

ESSEX TRADING COMPANY –
www.essextrading.com, for important futures software products and much more.

COMMODITY FUTURES TRADING CLUB –
www.commoditytraders.com, for commodity futures traders or those wishing to learn about or get started in commodity futures trading.

INVESTOR'S BUSINESS DAILY –
www.investors.com, review the latest business news online.

Free 2 Week Trial Offer for U.S. Residents From Investor's Business Daily:

INVESTOR'S BUSINESS DAILY will provide you with the facts, figures, and objective news analysis you need to succeed.

Investor's Business Daily is formatted for a quick and concise read to help you make informed and profitable decisions.

To take advantage of this free 2 week trial offer,
e-mail us at customerservice@traderslibrary.com
or visit our website at www.traderslibrary.com where
you find other free offers as well.

You can also reach us by calling 1-800-272-2855
or fax us at 410-964-0027.

This book, along with other books, are available at discounts that make it realistic to provide them as gifts to your customers, clients, and staff. For more information on these long lasting, cost effective premiums, please call John Boyer at 800-424-4550 or email him at john@traderslibrary.com.

About the Author and Essex Trading Company, Ltd.

Jay Kaeppel is the Director of Research at Essex Trading Company, Ltd. and an active Commodity Trading Advisor (CTA). With over 12 years of futures trading and system development experience, his expertise as a system developer has been noted by Technical Analysis of Stocks and Commodities magazine, which has published several of his articles on such diverse topics as:

- A Winning Approach to Futures Trading *
- Stock market timing with interest rates
- Stock market timing with the Stock/Bond Yield Gap
- Stock market timing with long-term price momentum
- Bond mutual fund investing and bond market timing *
- Gold mutual fund investing and gold market timing *

Jay Kaeppel is the subject of an interview in the May 1997 issue of *Technical Analysis of Stocks and Commodities* magazine, discussing stock market timing, stock selection techniques, trading system development and futures and option trading.

"Formula Research," a national monthly trading system development advisory edited by Nelson Freeburg has acknowledged Jay Kaeppel's expertise as a trading systems developer by using two of his original systems as the foundation of their own stock market and gold fund trading systems.

Copies of these articles are available on the Essex Trading Company website.

Essex Trading Company, Ltd. has been a leading developer of trading software for futures and option traders since 1983. Essex Trading Group, a division of Essex Trading Company, Ltd. is registered with the National Futures Association as a Commodity Trading Advisor and has been managing money since 1995. The President of Essex Trading Company, Ltd. is David Wesolowicz, a veteran trader with over 9 years of experience as a floor trader on the Chicago Board Options Exchange and the Chicago Board of Trade. Mr. Wesolowicz has over 16 years experience as a developer of software for trading applications. Together, Wesolowicz and Kaeppel have developed several software programs, most notably the award-winning Futures Pro and Option Pro On-Line programs.

COMPANY INFORMATION:

Essex Trading Company, Ltd.

107 North Hale, Suite 206

Wheaton, IL 60187

Phone: 800-726-2140 ext. 155 or 630-682-5780 ext. 155

Fax: 630-682-8065

E-mail address: essextr@aol.com

Internet Website address: http://www.essextrading.com

FREE DEMO DISK·
CALL TODAY!
800-272-2855
ext 155
BONUS: Get a $20 gift certificate to Traders' Library with your FREE Demo Disk